Exile's End –

a Memoir

by Frank Thomas Smith

ANTHROPOSOPHICAL PUBLICATIONS
FREMONT, MICHIGAN USA

EXILE'S END – A MEMOIR
By Frank Thomas Smith
© 2024 Frank Thomas Smith
https://SouthernCrossReview.org/

Published by
Anthroposophical Publications
Fremont, Michigan USA
https://AnthroposophicalPublications.org/

Author: Frank Thomas Smith
Illustrations: Celina MacKern
Editor: James D. Stewart

First edition
ISBN: 978-1-948302-61-6 paperback
978-1-948302-64-7 eBook

Printed in the United States of America

Table of Contents

Exile's End –
a Memoir

by Frank Thomas Smith

Exile's End

My faraway home is a land of lovers.
A greeting there is no touch of the hand,
No nod of the head, no Guten Tag, Herr *...*
In that distant land my friends all embrace me
And kiss me and tell me: Estás en tu casa.
A cleansing wind blows in from the Pampas,
It swirls even now in the streets of my mind ...
    ... to be continued.

In order to make an intelligent choice, or even a stupid one, you have to have reached a certain age, not necessarily a legal age, but at least one which allows thinking to function. On the other hand, according to some, including myself, your spirit exists both before birth and after death. And during the time between death and the future birth you train for the big moment, which includes choosing your future parents. If your future parents live in Brooklyn, NY as mine did, you will necessarily be born there — as I was. This implies that I made my first choice (possibly influenced by previous events and choices, intelligent or stupid) before I was even born. The way things turned out it was a very good choice. My parents were neither rich nor poor, originally working class, but after my father somehow became the U.S. sales representative for a Cuban tobacco company (before Castro), we at least approached middle class. When Castro took over Cuba the company lost its tobacco source, but the owners had moved their money and themselves to Florida. We stayed in Brooklyn and my father traveled a lot seeking tobacco in Mexico, and South and Central America. I had no sisters or brothers, don't know why. Neither my parents nor other relatives of that generation were intellectuals, nor did they have much faith in education, which they had lacked, having gone to work before finishing high school. So, they left me on my own in that respect.

What follows is a description of choices I have made during my life on earth. I have sometimes wondered to what extent they are strictly true. You may see what I mean by that from what follows. The descriptions are not necessarily or completely true, for memory is never exact and egotism tends to bend events to favor oneself.

I was born on October 23, 1932, in Brooklyn, New York, to Mabel Johnson and Alfred Smith. Mabel was born in New York City to Mabel McGlynn, of Irish extraction, and Harry Johnson, born in Norway with a Norwegian name later anglicized as Harry Johnson — known in the Lower East Side of Manhattan as "Dutch Harry." There is some doubt concerning my father's place of birth. I, and everyone else, assumed it was in the United States, but when my cousin Barbara investigated the family tree, she concluded that he had been born in England and arrived in the U.S. as a two-year-old infant. Both his parents — Gertrude Wellman and Francis Smith — were English immigrants. My grandfather became a captain in the New York national guard during the Second World War, something a working-class Brit like him could never have dreamed of becoming back on the old sod. I can still see the large photo of him in his captain's uniform on their living room wall.

My name at birth was Francis Smith. (I have a baptismal certificate to prove it.) When an adult and for a while a student of astrology, I worried if I was really a Scorpio, October 23rd being on the cusp of Libra. I asked my mother exactly when I was born, and she told me nine-thirty P.M. in Greenpoint Hospital. That made me definitely a Scorpio because 9:30 P.M. Brooklyn time was already 0:30 A.M October 24 Greenwich Mean Time. What a relief! I mean who wants to be a Libra who can't make up his mind about anything, especially choices.

You may have noticed that Francis Smith is not the name I use as the author of this memoir. I owe you an explanation if you've gotten this far. When I was about fourteen years old, my father took me on a business trip to Havana, Cuba, for which I needed a passport, for which I needed a birth certificate. I went to the Board of Health, where they keep such documents. I told the lady who attended to me that I was born on October 23, 1932, in Greenpoint Hospital, Brooklyn and I wanted a copy of my birth certificate. After having retreated to the inner sanctum of files, she came back to me and said that on that date only a "baby boy Smith" was born. I guess they forgot to register my name, it happens sometimes. "What did you say your name is?"

I saw an opportunity. I never liked having Francis for a name, for it sounded exactly like the girl's name, Frances. Everyone called me Frank or Frankie anyway. Also, it was only a year or two after World War Two and my hero was my uncle Tom, who had been a sergeant in the army having fought from Africa through Italy to victory. I told the lady that my name was Frank Thomas Smith. The lady yawned, put a paper in her typewriter and typed me out a cool birth certificate, signed, stamped, sealed and handed over. Thus, Baby boy Smith became Frank Thomas Smith. Good choice.

Holy Innocents

When reading the following event, you may think, "What's the big deal here? The choice was obvious." Nowadays maybe, but please understand that way back then morality mores were different. Clark Gable caused a sensation when he said, "I don't give a damn, Scarlet," in *Gone With the Wind*. Sex was unseen and unheard in movies; even double beds couldn't be shown because it implied that people of the opposite sex slept together, let alone same-sex couples, who were unmentionable. Furthermore, I had been brought up a Roman Catholic. My parents were far from practicing, they preferred to sleep in their double bed to going to mass Sunday mornings. But my Aunt Gertie decided to save my soul before it was too late. She dragged me to mass every Sunday and Holy Days of Obligation. I also had to attend religious instruction for First Communion. I'd had it drummed into me that messing around with sex was seriously sinful and dangerous to body and soul — although there was little opportunity for playtime with the opposite sex because girls were even more terrified than boys of mortal damnation, also-known-as eternity in hell.

Ironically, it was Bill Desmond who started the whole thing, probably because he was older and more interested in sex stuff than the rest of the kids. It wasn't that we weren't interested, it's just that we hadn't realized how interested we were until Bill brought it up. Bill called a meeting at the basement entrance of the last building in the row of apartments we all lived in on East 22nd Street in the Flatbush section of Brooklyn. The entrance led down a short flight of steps into the basement, so if we sat on the steps, we couldn't be seen by grownups passing by, although hardly any passed by there anyway. There were Bill and Simon and me: the boys, and Muriel, Miriam and Janet: the girls. Muriel was born sexy, not that she *was* sexy, but she was very interested in sex. Like when we played our brand of Leap Frog, when one kid would stand back against the wall and the next kid would bend over and put his or her shoulder against his or her waist and the others would form a line by putting their heads under the ass and between the legs of the kid in front until a line of five or six bent-over kids was formed that looked like a giant worm caught on a hook. Then the first kid

4

of the other team would run and leap up over the line and land as far up on the worms back as possible. Then the next until if all of the opposing team was able to jump on the worm and not fall off and the worm didn't break, the worm won; if it did break under the pressure the opposing team won. Our parents thought it was good clean fun. Whenever I got to stick my head under Muriel's ass, she started to squirm around on my neck and, if the game lasted long enough, wet my collar. What a smell, wow! But she was homely and had braces on her teeth. Miriam was Puerto Rican, at least her parents were, and she was born there. She was sexy too, but she was scared shitless of her father, who would have beaten her to an inch of her life if he ever heard what we were up to. She was kind of pretty, but her nose was too big.

Janet was different, dark, beautiful and shy and we were all secretly in love with her. I say secretly because no boy at that age would dare to admit that he had anything more than a passing interest in girls. You know how it is. Janet kept still when your head was under her ass and she didn't wiggle around when she jumped on your back either, like Muriel did.

Bill had the habit of scratching his pimples when he was nervous. He scratched his ass, too, which meant that he probably had pimples there as well. His proposal was simple, direct and exhilarating. He wanted to look at the girls' sex organs; in exchange, they could look at ours. (He also informed us that Chinese girls pussies were horizontal, whereas white girls' pussies were vertical.) We all sort of sat there with our mouths hanging open, turning various shades of pink. But no one said no, so Bill went on. We should think of some place to go, like one of the apartment house cellars (he had one in mind) and just look. He made it sound scientific. Simon, to everyone's surprise, was the first to agree, albeit monosyllabically: "When?" Bill, who had never said a kind word to Simon until that moment, patted him on the shoulder. "Soon," he said, "right now if you want." This was the moment when I had to choose — to risk eternity in hell in exchange for a glimpse of some female pussies — one in particular. I chose the glimpse. (whew!)

"I don't want to go into no cellar," Janet said demurely. What did she mean — that she didn't want to do it at all, or she only didn't want to do it in a cellar? I wanted to say something so they wouldn't hear my heart beating, but I couldn't think of anything, so I just stared at Janet's knees, pressed firmly together, imagining what wonders lay north of them.

"It don't have to be no cellar," Muriel said. "Light's no good anyway."

"We could take a flashlight," Bill insisted.

"Your parents both work, Miriam," Muriel, who didn't like the cellar idea much either, said. "How about your place?"

"Oh no," Miriam gulped, "my father would kill me if he found out."

"Why should he find out?"

"Leave her alone if she don't want to ..." Simon began.

"I don't not want to, just not in my place," Miriam said and blushed scarlet under her olive skin.

"I'll think of something," Bill offered. "The question is if you all want to." He looked at the girls one by one, taking it for granted that we boys certainly wanted to. The only girl who hadn't agreed emphatically was Janet, but she was the most important one, possessing the tropical Shangri-La between her legs that we all wanted to examine, if only from a respectable distance. "I don't know," she said. "I gotta think about it."

"What about right here" Simon said eagerly, "now?"

"Are you crazy?" Bill admonished and punched him on the same shoulder he had fondly patted a minute before. "Any one of those

6

windows could open" — he pointed upward with his thumb at four stories of apartments above us — "and we'd be seen. Shut your stupid trap if you can't say nothing intelligent."

"I gotta think about it," Janet repeated and stood up from the step she'd been sitting on and smoothed out her cute little skirt. (Girls wore skirts then, remember?) I gotta go home now."

"Me too," Miriam said, and followed Janet around to the front of the building. The rest of us sat there a while deep in dirty thoughts, until Muriel, realizing she was the only girl left, jumped up and yelled, "Hey, wait for me," and ran after them.

Bill sneezed three times hard and held his head. "Jeez, I got a headache."

The next morning, Saturday, Simon rang my bell at eight o'clock. I was up already; in fact, I woke up at six o'clock and couldn't get back to sleep for thinking about what we were planning and if anything would come of it. My parents were sleeping, and my father yelled: "Who the hell is that?" I told him it was only Simon and I had to go out. He grumbled something and went back to sleep.

"I couldn't hardly sleep all night," Simon said as we ran down the three flights of stairs. "Do you think the girls will do it?"

"Do what?" I was trying to seem calm about it.

"You know, *it*, what Bill said."

"How should I know?" Then, after letting Simon suffer a while, "They seemed pretty hot to go, though. At least Muriel and Miriam."

"What do you think we should do?"

"About what?"

"About finding out whether they're gonna do it."

"Ask them, I guess."

"Yeah," Simon grinned. "Should we go ring their bells?"

7

"Nah, that'd be suspicious. They'll come out. It's Saturday."

"What about Bill?"

"What about him?

"Does he have to know?"

"It was his idea."

"Yeah, but he's a pain in the ass."

"And he'll bust our asses if we try to do it without him."

That convinced Simon that Bill couldn't be avoided, so we went to his apartment and rang the bell. His mother opened the door: "Yeah?"

"Can Bill come out?" I asked her.

"Bill's sick, I think he's got the flu or somethin', though I don't know how he could have the flu in summer."

That was too bad, but I never saw a happier kid than Simon. Actually, I was glad too, because Bill *was* a pain in the ass, although he sometimes had good ideas. We hung around for an hour or so until the other kids started coming out. We kept by ourselves though, like we had a secret, which we did. Finally, Miriam appeared.

"Should we ask her if she wants to do it alone?" Simon asked.

"Nah, she'll never do it alone. Let's ask her to get Muriel and Janet."

Simon ran up to her before she could get involved in something with the other kids and said, "Hey, Miriam, how about gettin' hold of Janet and Muriel?" She didn't ask why, she knew. She ran to Muriel's building first and about five minutes later we saw the two of them running to Janet's building, and after another five minutes the three of them came sashaying out arm in arm. Simon and I put our hands in our pockets and walked towards them, not directly of course, kind of diagonally, and at the last minute we swerved as though we'd just thought of something and intercepted them.

"Hey," Simon said, his face all red. "How about doin' it?" which was probably the worst thing he could have said.

"Doing *what*?" Janet said, looking at me instead of Simon with her big black eyes and throwing her hair back. God, she was beautiful.

"Ahr ... what Simon means is doing what we talked about yesterday."

"Where's Bill?" Muriel asked, looking like she wanted to drop her panties right then and there.

"Bill's sick, can't come," Simon explained anxiously, "but that don't matter, we're here."

"That makes us three to you two," Muriel said, probably disappointed at having one less pecker to look at.

"Good," Janet said. "I'm not about to show anything to *him* anyway."

"You're right, Janet, absolutely right," Simon almost panted. "He's a pain in the ass."

"Watch your language," Janet said, frowning.

"Yeah, watch your language," Muriel repeated. Simon looked like he didn't know what language they meant and didn't say anything, which was just as well.

"But where?" Miriam asked. "Not in my house, that's for sure."

They'd obviously already decided to go for it but were still worried about the place. My mouth was dryer than the Sahara Desert, but I knew I had to talk fast. "You know, the perfect place just occurred to me." Like Hell! I'd been thinking about it since six o'clock in the morning. They say that inspiration hits when you just wake up and that's what happened to me. They were all looking at me expectantly.

"The church around the corner," I whispered, leaning close to the girls.

"The Protestant one?" Miriam asked.

"That's the only one around the corner."

Janet, Miriam and I were Catholics and Muriel and Simon were Jewish, so we couldn't have cared less about a Protestant church. In fact, it was the perfect place to sin. There weren't many Protestants in Brooklyn those days, probably still aren't, so they came from all around to go to that church. All doomed to hell for being Protestants, while we Catholics could go to confession any time and get to heaven eventually. Muriel and Simon would probably go to the same place as the Protestants, but that was their business.

"The church is locked on Saturdays," Janet said sensibly.

"I don't mean *inside* the church, I mean in these pits they have in front of the basement windows." They all knew what I meant. In order for the basement meeting hall to have natural light, rectangular cavities had been cut into the ground and iron railings put around them so no one would fall in. They were swell hiding places in games when you had to hide, and we had all used them for that purpose until everyone knew about them and they had become too obvious for hide and seek.

"Yeah, that's perfect, Frankie!" Simon exclaimed, beside himself with excitement.

"They're kinda small for all of us," Janet said.

"With Bill, yes," I agreed, "but we're not so many now."

"Let's just take a look," Muriel said. Good old Muriel.

"OK, but I still don't know," Janet said, looking at me again.

"Let's go," Simon said and started down the street. "C'mon!"

"No," Janet said. "You boys go the other way, around to Ditmas Avenue. We'll go this way." See how smart she was?

"Sure," Simon agreed. "And we'll meet there."

Janet strode off quickly with the other girls at her heels. Simon was hopping up and down in place, "C'mon, Frankie."

"Don't run," I admonished him, "everybody'll be looking at us."

"Hey, Frankie," one of the other boys yelled. "Where ya goin'? We're gettin' up a game of stickball."

"Nowhere," I answered over my shoulder, and Simon and I walked as casually as we could in the opposite direction from the one the girls had taken. Once we'd turned the corner, though, we broke into a trot, then a gallop, turned the other corner and finally came to the church. The girls were nowhere in sight.

"Do you think they chickened out?" Simon asked, biting his nails.

"Nah, they're walkin'." We ran, that's all. A minute later they turned the corner and approached us, Muriel and Miriam ahead and Janet now hanging back a step or two. Simon and I entered the churchyard cemetery, passed the time-worn tombstones (it was one of the oldest churches in America) and waited at the railing of one of the cavities. It was a perfect spot, well protected by two tall chestnut trees. When the girls came into the cemetery, we climbed over the railing and jumped into the cavity. We looked through the meeting hall window just in case, but it was empty. "C'mon down," Simon whispered hoarsely to the three girls peering down at us like full moons.

Muriel and Miriam were ready to climb over the railing, I'm sure, but Janet said, "I'm not going down *there*." She had class, you see.

"But how we gonna do it if you don't come down?" Simon pleaded.

"From up here," Janet said.

"Oh."

"You first," Muriel said, meaning us.

Simon fumbled with his fly and finally got his dick out. He was so nervous he didn't even have a hard-on and it looked real puny there in his palm. I was nervous, too, but I had half a hard-on at least. We looked up and saw them gazing down at us with what I can only call a mixture of interest and amusement. Passion? Not that I could tell. I guess they were nervous too. Suddenly Muriel spread her legs like a cowgirl getting ready to draw and pulled her panties to one side with two fingers, revealing an incipient black bush of pubic hair. Muriel did the same and we could see her pussy real well, because it was covered with a transparent mantle of blonde hair. We stared at Janet's knees. Finally, she shrugged, took up the cowgirl stance, placed two fingers on her crotch and pulled aside her panties.

It was gorgeous, a plume of shiny dark hair with a crease in the middle that allowed the essence of her pulchritude to shine through like a purple sun. Our jaws dropped and Simon's dick began to grow and glow like a sausage with special effects. Mine had long since reached epic adolescent proportions. But the revelation lasted only a few seconds. Janet released her fingers and the panties snapped back into place eclipsing the sun. The other girls followed suit and they all turned and left. Simon and I lay there primed to the gills. I won't mention what we did then; I guess you can imagine.

At nine the next morning, Sunday, the phone rang. It was Simon. "Meeting in a half hour, same place, the girls are coming," was all he said in a voice that sounded like he was gasping for air. I got dressed and was waiting at the meeting place when the others arrived. Simon got right to the point.

"It was real good, I mean doing it, yesterday." He was still panting for air. "Now I think we should do it again, but ... but ... but this time you girls come down with us, one by one or in twos if you think there's enough room, and this time we *touch* too."

We all gaped at him. A second later it came to me in a flash. Simon wanted to utilize all of the five senses that we had learned about in school. We'd already *seen*, now we would *touch*. Was there anything to *hear*? I didn't see how there could be, but you never know. But next would come *smell* and I knew from when I had my head between Muriel's legs playing leapfrog that there was something to smell. And *taste*? I pulled a curtain down over my mind. It was too much to even contemplate. No one said anything. Were the girls having the same thoughts? No, I couldn't believe that they were as perverse as us.

"It'd be easy," Simon went on, still gasping, "you take off your panties instead of just holding them aside and ...

"You sinful boy ...!" Our hearts boomed in unison as we looked up and saw Mrs. McIntyre leaning out her first-floor window with yellow curlers in her hair waving her fist down at us. *"Get out of here with your filth."* We stood up and ran, girls in one direction, boys in the other. Her parting words reached me like an arrow piercing my heart: "And I'm gonna tell YOUR mother!" Simon and I stopped running three blocks away and leaned against a lamppost, panting. "Sinful boy," she said. Who'd she mean?"

"You, Simon," I said, worried that he wanted to pin it on me. "You were the one doing the talking."

"Yeah, that's what I think, too. Whose mother do you think she meant? She didn't say mothers, did she?

"No, but she might've meant it."

"Yeah. Janet's at least, they go to mass and novenas and all that crap together."

I nodded. "Poor Janet. She won't tell Miriam's mother though. She don't talk to Pordaricans."

"No," Simon agreed. "She don't talk to Jews neither if she can help it, the old bitch, so that leaves Muriel and me off the hook."

"Yeah, but I'm Catlick."

"Yeah," Simon sighed. "Anyway, I guess that's the end of *it*."

That night the phone rang at home and Mom answered in the bedroom: "Yes, Mrs. McIntyre, how are you? ... Oh? (long pause) ... Really? ... ... (long pause) ... ... Yes, certainly, thank you for calling, Mrs. McIntyre." Mom came into the living room where I was reading a comic and stood for a second before me. I dared to look up in time to see a faint smile on her face as she turned and walked into the kitchen. That's when I learned for the first time what a great Mom I had.

We didn't see the girls right away, Janet because she got hell and was dragged off to confession immediately at Holy Innocents, the Catholic Church nearest to us, about ten blocks away, and the other two because they weren't allowed to come out. When Bill got better, he wanted to take up where he left off, so we had to tell him what happened. At first, he was furious that we had gone on without him, but when he heard about Mrs. McIntyre yelling at Simon that he was a sinful boy, he laughed and said, "Sinful Simon, that's who you are." The name stuck and was soon shortened to just plain "Sin," which is what everyone called him from then on.

Brooklyn Prep

Sometimes you make a choice that fails. The result may be positive or negative or simply meaningless. The failure of this choice was positive, although I didn't realize it until much later.

14

Upon graduating from elementary school, P.S. 152, I applied for admission to Brooklyn Preparatory High School. I don't remember why, although it was probably because some friend convinced me that it was cool and small and had a good but humble football team. It was located in downtown Brooklyn, so would require a trolley-bus trip to and from every day. This didn't bother me, on the contrary I rather looked forward to it. I had to take an admission test, which didn't bother me either, because until then I had found school examinations easy. Much later I came to suspect that the teachers who prepared them feared their teaching ability would appear incompetent if many students failed, in the public schools at least.

I remember only one question on the Brooklyn Prep test — in mathematics or, rather, arithmetic — that I had a problem with. It asked to solve a half dozen square roots — numbers with a symbol that looks like a fishhook ($\sqrt{}$). I had no idea how to do that, most likely because I was playing hooky on the day we learned about square roots in P.S. 152. Just to put something, I divided all the numbers by two, knowing it was incorrect. A week or two later, I received a letter from the school informing me that I had passed the test with around 75% (I think), but because their system is competitive, I would not be admitted to the school. Just for spite I never did learn how to calculate square roots, beyond guessing, which worked for small numbers, but not for high ones. Today it's a piece of cake for computers.

It was a choice that failed — apparently, but in a positive way for my future. I later (much later) discovered that Brooklyn Prep was a Catholic school run by Jesuits.

"Brooklyn Preparatory School, commonly referred to as Brooklyn Prep, was a highly selective Jesuit preparatory school founded by the Society of Jesus in 1908. The school educated generations of young men from throughout New

York City and Long Island until its closure in 1972. As a Jesuit institution, Brooklyn Prep was noted for its religious values, classical roots (e.g. Latin and Greek), and dress code (ties and jackets) — all part of its goal of turning out well-rounded, educated men ... But whether a student could solve algebraic equations with unusual facility or consistently throw cross body blocks that led to touchdowns, he submitted as a prepster to an iron, relentless discipline ..." (New York Times — 1972).

Obviously, it was not my cup of tea. Furthermore, if I had studied there, I might well have become a fanatical Roman Catholic, perhaps even a priest, a bishop, even a pope instead of the Argentine Jorge Bergoglio, who calls himself Francisco. I wouldn't even have had to change my name. Now, in case you think that I, as pope, would redeem a dying medieval institution by allowing women to become priests, kicking out sexually abusive priests, throwing the myth of celibacy overboard, etc., you might be disappointed, given that I could have been successfully brainwashed by the Jesuits of Brooklyn Prep and kept things as they still are, or worse. Oh, the gods of Jesuitism don't give up so easily. They tried again at university level.

The University of Vermont

Why I went to the University of Vermont, of all places, is hard to explain, even to myself. My friend Jerry (his real name), a year or two older than me, who went there and told me how great it was and that he would get me into the best national fraternity, was certainly an influence, for I would never even have heard of it otherwise. Also, it was a time when Brooklyn College, where I should have gone, was determining admission by an examination. Perhaps I was still traumatized by having failed the entrance examination for Brooklyn Prep. To make the choice even more

16

absurd, I applied for the college of agriculture. Why? Because I had just seen a movie with Alan Ladd about farming and combines and crooks who Alan, a courageous farmer, defeats and wins the farmer's daughter. Or maybe I just wanted to get away from home, which seems illogical though, because my parents were not at all domineering, rather the opposite. They were non-academic types, having skipped high school in favor of or need to work. If I wanted to go to the U. of Vermont, of all places, why not?

I was thoroughly miserable in the so-called city of Burlington, the frozen apple of Vermont, down the hill from the university. Compared to the big apple core of the civilized world, New York, it was Deadsville, dry as a bone. I turned eighteen in October and couldn't even get a legal beer without buying a meal to go with it. I also realized how deficient my high school education had been. As an agriculture major, I naturally had a course in chemistry, something I had not the slightest idea about, not having studied it in high school. (I am still abysmally ignorant of chemistry, by the way.) My knowledge of mathematics was sketchy, to say the least. About the only subject I liked and did well in was English literature. What made the University of Vermont bearable was football. I made the freshman team and would surely have gone on to the varsity team in a year or two, except for a blow to the side of my head. (We wore leather helmets those days.) It caused an infection in my right earlobe, eventually a cyst. Prompt medical attention might have taken care of it, but my guardian angel must have whispered into that ear, "Let it Be." It ended my football career and, indirectly and eventually, my incipient academic career. I still have the cyst to remind me.

Then there was the restaurant in Burlington where students liked to hang out. I forget its name, so I'll call it Jane's. Jane was the Saturday night waitress. Whenever I had enough pocket money I'd walk downtown to Jane's, order a bottle of beer and a hamburger, the latter enabling me to repeat the beer order ad infinitum. One

Saturday night I walked the waitress home, intending to seduce her. As it turned out she, experienced, seduced me, the novice. A few days later I was visiting a fellow football player in his dorm room. He was a bruising tackle. Above his bed, as though it were a painting, a real waitress apron was pinned. Under it the beast had written, in black crayon, "manhole cover." I was shocked, embarrassed, angry. I left the room as soon as possible, and never returned. If I remember correctly, I didn't return to Jane's either.

In another place, a diner, I met Bill Este one night. He was a few years older than me, getting educated on his veteran's benefits. We got talking over hamburgers and beer about Dostoevsky, especially *The Brothers Karamazov*. Bill was surprised not only that I had heard of it, but that I had actually *read* it. I read a lot, thanks to the New York Public Library having a branch in Brooklyn where we lived. That branch wasn't very big, and it didn't have many books, but if you wanted something, they'd get it for you in a week from the central library on Fifth Avenue in Manhattan.

Bill and I thought ourselves to be intellectually superior, because we were probably the only students in UVM who had read Dostoevsky — or had even heard of him. Finally, after meeting a few times more with conversation and beer, we agreed that the U. of Vermont was inferior to our talents (despite my imminent failing in chemistry and mathematics). Bill had a plan, a solution. He said he had only decided to enroll in UVM because the skiing was said to be so good. Well, it was already November, and it hadn't even snowed yet. And it was bitter cold. Bill suggested that we abandon Vermont and transfer to Georgetown University in Washington DC. He knew important people there, he claimed, and he could get us both accepted. We could leave the next morning. He had a Volkswagen Beetle, which I admired almost as much as I did him. He said we could share driving and be there in a couple of days. In order to understand why I agreed to this crazy plan, you must know that I had consumed an inordinate quantity of beer and was, to be honest, drunk. Bill said he'd call for me in the lobby of my dorm at eight o'clock the next morning. "Be ready!" he ordered. The next morning, a Saturday, my roommate, a Vermont hick, shook me awake. There's a guy outside looking for you, he said.

"Let's go, Frankie," Bill Este said. I remembered last night through the haze of a hangover and looked at him numbly.

"You coming, or not?" he said, clearly angry. I thought about what I'd tell my parents, that I just decided to take a trip to Washington DC in a VW beetle with an older guy I barely knew. I made a choice. "Er ... no, Bill, I changed my mind," I mumbled weakly. He seemed to want to say something, but just turned on his heel and left. I never saw him again. It was a good choice. I found out later that Georgetown was and still is a Jesuit university that supplies the government with many of its most powerful politicians, as well as the Supreme Court.

The Jesuit order relied on the plantations and slave labor to sustain the clergy and to help finance the construction and the day-to-day operations of churches and schools, including Georgetown, the nation's first Catholic institution of higher learning. [Wikipedia]

I had escaped again by the skin of my teeth. Maybe it was the proverbial last straw, in that it cut off an avenue of escape from the cold, the hillbillies, chemistry, math and, worst blow of all, the end of my football career. I went home by train on the Christmas break and proved to my eighteen-year-old-self that there's no place like home. I told my parents that I didn't want to go back to Vermont (good choice) and they just shrugged. My dad asked about all my stuff that was still up there and I said I'd just have to go back and get it. "Let's drive up there and get it," he said. "You can drive." I had turned eighteen in October, so the first thing I had done on arriving in Brooklyn was applying for and obtaining my driver's license — thanks to my dad, who had taught me to drive.

So, we drove up to Burlington in his Hudson Hornet. (That was before General Motors and Ford bought or forced out all the smaller competition.) I went right to my room in the dorm and told my roommate — a hick farmer, but a nice guy — that I was leaving for good and to please tell whomever it may concern that I'm gone. He stared at me with bulging eyes and open mouth while watching me pack. Finally, he asked if I wanted help, which I did, so he carried one of my two suitcases down to the car. We shook hands (boys didn't embrace those days) and that was it.

Agnes (on my right) beautiful and intelligent, was my first girlfriend. Being a true Catholic virgin, it was a chaste relationship. We were about 18. This could have been in Coney Island.

General Cover Underwriters

I roved around for a while in Brooklyn, had a couple of jobs delivering newspapers (The Brooklyn Eagle) and meat and vegetables (Abe & Ben's Kosher Market), but finally decided I should get more serious, so looked up the help wanted ads in the newspapers. An employment agency sent me to an insurance company to apply for a job as "assistant underwriter." Besides not knowing anything about insurance, I didn't even know what an "underwriter" is, except that it sounds like underwater. I asked the employment agency guy, but he didn't know either. He told me not to worry about it, that the General Cover company was desperate for a young white All-American male, relatively intelligent, with a high school education, no experience necessary, assistant underwriter trainee, and I filled the bill, at least according to him. "They'll tell you what an underwriter is, and you can tell me."

General Cover Underwriters occupied a whole floor in a skyscraper on Wall Street. I was interviewed first by a vice-president, then by a supervisor named George Fellows, who asked me three easy questions and told me I was hired, starting immediately. He turned me over to Bob, who shook hands and sat me, almost physically, at "my" desk, complete with swivel chair, blotter, telephone and a device I couldn't identify. It turned out to be a voice recorder that I used to write letters. Once a few letters were recorded, I ejected the recording and carried it down to the other end of the floor to the typing pool occupied by a dozen or so women, mostly young, because female ambition those days seldom amounted to more than getting married and staying home to mind the children.

George was supervisor of the New York City and Kentucky regions. What, you may ask, does NYC have to do with Kentucky? Nothing directly, but they were the two most lucrative insurance regions — New York because it was the center of the universe and Kentucky because it was the center and the periphery of the whiskey industry. (Whiskey warehouses were highly inflammable.) I had the fourth desk from George's glass office in a horizontal row. In front of me were twelve horizontal rows of backs of heads. Each row was responsible for one or more regions of the country. We, however, were the most important ones. My future career and life were clear: in about ten years I'd be a full underwriter. (To underwrite something is to guarantee that an insurance policy will pay in case of accident or death, ergo an insurance company. So, an underwriter is someone who advises the insurance company that it's worth the risk or not, my own definition.) Meanwhile I would get married, have kids, thus be stuck in the boring life I'd just stepped into. Heavy drinking with the boys (colleagues), affairs with typing pool girls, etc. A Choice was necessary.

The Army

The Korean War was fought between North Korea and South Korea from 1950 to 1953. The war began on 25 June 1950 when North Korea invaded South Korea following clashes along the border and rebellions in South Korea. North Korea was supported by China and the Soviet Union while South Korea was supported by the United States and allied countries. The fighting ended with an armistice on 27 July 1953.

A military "draft," a.k.a. conscription, was in effect in the United States and I was a prime subject to soon become a draftee — eighteen years old with no responsibilities except myself. In fact, I was expecting the draftee notification at any moment, but it didn't come. So, I decided to make it happen. I knew how, it was called voluntary conscription, a contradiction in terms if there ever was one. The difference between it and enlistment as such was that enlistment was for four years, and conscription, voluntary or forced, was for eighteen months. My choice was to go for it. One of the luckiest choices I ever made.

Please don't think the choice was due to misguided patriotism, I don't think so anyway. The excuse I made to myself was that I was tired of waiting. But in reality, it involved a small dose of existential angst. What I was tired of was a feeling that my life was being wasted on a boring job and a blurred future. The loss of a girlfriend may have had something to do with it as well. I was "going steady" with Patricia, a pretty Catholic girl (weren't they all?) who didn't dare to "go all the way" (didn't they all?). Those days the only way to get there was by marriage.

One day I went unannounced to her home, a few blocks from my own in Brooklyn, for some reason I don't recall. It must have been a weekend. I rang the bell and after a short wait Patricia herself answered with swollen eyes, puffy cheeks, messy hair, dressed in wrinkled, unsightly pajamas. When she saw it was me, she gasped, stepped back and slammed the door. She phoned me a few hours later and explained that she had a bad cold and would be unavailable for a few days. When she did reappear, she was indeed rejuvenated and as pretty as before. Nevertheless, it had been a devastating revelation for me that she, a nearly angelic being, could actually be subject to colds and a runny nose and, God forbid, constipation. Our "steady going" ended wordlessly.

It may well be that my real motivation was simply boredom with life as I was living it, or (don't throw your computer at the wall) — karma. All I had to do was go to the draft board, somewhere downtown, and sign something. Much to my disappointment nobody there seemed particularly interested in my voluntary conscription. Nobody even asked *why*. A week later I received a letter in the mail instructing me to report somewhere (downtown again, but not the same place) for induction in the U.S. Army. I said goodbye to my weeping mom and my stern-faced dad and simply left with the clothes on my back and the few things the letter allowed me to take. I was there almost all day on lines waiting for a physical examination, and what turned out to be an all-important IQ test.

Finally, I was standing on my last line of the day, waiting to board a bus taking us somewhere — hopefully not directly to Korea. I glanced across the street and was surprised, almost shocked to see my father standing there watching. He wore his usual gray suit with tie and vest and fedora hat. I broke ranks — well, not exactly a "rank" — and crossed the street to him. We didn't embrace. C'mon, that was New York in the early nineteen-fifties. Men didn't *embrace*. We shook hands. He mumbled something about good luck, I guess, I don't really remember. But I do remember that I was moved by his gesture of just showing up there, I mean he wasn't that kind of guy. And he was the only one! Someone whistled for me, and I ran back and boarded the bus. I waved to my dad as we pulled out. "Anyone know where we're going?" someone called out. "Maybe it's a secret," someone else said.

A few hours later we pulled into Fort Dix in New Jersey. All I remember about that place is that they gave us uniforms and shots against diseases I never heard of, and they had us cutting officers' lawns. After a couple of days some of us boarded another bus, this time an overnight journey to Fort Breckinridge in Kentucky — and things began to get interesting. The first shock was that we were in Company A, 101 Airborne Infantry Division. When we saw that sign over the door of the Company HQ, we almost fainted — figuratively of course. I ain't jumpin outta some airplane, someone yelled. We learned that 101 Airborne Division — also known as the Screaming Eagle — was now in a basic training mode, so we wouldn't be jumping any time soon.

The war in Korea wasn't going very well at that time, something even those of us who kept up with the news weren't aware of because actual news reports, that is, those that told the public the truth, were far and in between those days. That meant that there

EXILE'S END — A MEMOIR

were very few noncoms and officers around to train new guys like us because they were so badly needed in Korea. In fact, we only had the Company Commander, a lieutenant who was really a lawyer. Then there was First Sergeant Jackson, a battle-scarred veteran who was in Hawaii when the Japs attacked. He ran the company, but I guess First Sergeants run most companies. The Field First Sergeant was Silas Taylor, a wiry little guy from Georgia who had spent a lot of time in Korea, was wounded a few times, and even had a Silver Star. I was really surprised — we all were — to learn that he was only twenty-one years old, because he had eyes that looked a lot older. There were no more noncoms, except for Sgt. Alphabet, who ran the quartermaster section, so didn't really count. On our first day Sgt. Taylor asked if anyone had military experience. No one had, but one guy was a cop in civilian life, so they made him Acting Platoon Leader. Another guy was a lifeguard at Jones Beach, so they made him one too. And so on. I thought of mentioning that I had been a Boy Scout but decided not to. They probably would have made me Acting Company Commander.

One day during the first week, Sgt. First Class Silas Taylor ran us up a hill. He went first and got there about a hundred yards before the first trainee. We struggled up puffing and groaning and Sgt. Taylor waited until the last one arrived before he began his speech, which went something like this, after telling us to "light 'em up those that got 'em and relax." Those days everyone smoked so everyone who had 'em lit 'em up.

"Ah said *run* up this here hill and you pussies didn't run, you *crawled*." He didn't shout, just talked loud enough in his Southern accent for all of us to hear. Some of us had never even heard a Southern accent before, except in the movies. "Now, if y'all keep doin' things that I tell y'all to do like that, I mean crawlin' instead a runnin', your gonna be fuckin' *me*, cause ahm supposed to get this here company in shape to go over and fight the enemy. That means *you-all*. In shape! Now ah don't like to be fucked, and if y'all fuck me, I'm gonna fuck *you-all*. And you can bet your sweet asses that I can fuck y'all better than y'all can fuck me. On the other hand, if y'all do what ah says, and do it *like* ah says, y'all will not have any problems in this here company. Is-that-understood? Silence. Answer me, goddammittafuckinhell!" He did shout the last word, if you can call it a word. "Yes, Sergeant," someone mumbled. "Louder! *All* a yuh!" He made us say it louder about five times until we were screaming. "OK, now we're goin' down the hill and we're *runnin'*. If any a you city slickers don't know what runnin' means, I'm telling ya. It means movin' *fast*."

He was as good as his word. A couple of wise guys who thought they could get away with goofing-off found themselves on a week of KP, one guy even got sent back to a new company and had to start basic all over again. And when we did things right, we sometimes got off some shit details or got weekend passes. He won our respect. He was fair and could do everything he made us do better than we could.

The problem with our first night-march was that Freddy Polanski, the medic, had the flu and couldn't go. Some thought that Freddy had some medical school because he was a pretty good medic, but I think he just took the three-day first aid course they give for medics because it was better than the rifle range or hiking up hills. It wasn't like in *Saving Private Ryan*, where the medic could perform a heart transplant on the battlefield. The second problem was Lieutenant Scumbag. I forget his real name, but that's what we called him. He simply appeared one day standing alongside Sgt. Taylor when we were in formation. Sgt. Taylor said this is Lt. Scumbag (he used his real name, naturally) and he'll be with us from now on. End of introduction.

"Who wants to be medic until Pvt. Polanski is back on his feet?" Sgt. Taylor asked. We had been in training for two months of the four-month course and had already learned the basic army rule: *never volunteer for anything*. But I wasn't sure that was always a good rule to live by. Look at Sy Abrams. On the first day they asked if anyone knew how to type. Sy raised his hand, and they made him Acting Company Clerk — no lying in the mud at the rifle range, no night marches, no KP. It was from Sy, by the way, that we learned about the argument between Sgt. Taylor and Lt. Scumbag. But I'll get to that later.

I raised my hand, volunteering to be medic. Sgt. Taylor was glad that he didn't have to ask if someone had medical experience and when no one answered just appoint somebody. "OK, Smith," he said, "Go get Polanski's stuff."

Every company has a medic and in combat he doesn't carry his full field equipment, only his first-aid kit and a light carbine rifle instead of the heavy M1. That's so he can run unimpeded to the wounded. His other stuff goes in the truck with the officers' things. As training is supposed to be as realistic as possible, our medic went lightly loaded, too. That's why I volunteered. Boy, did I think I was smart!

I'll tell you about the argument now. Just before the march, Lt. Scumbag, Field First Sgt. Taylor, and First Sgt. Jackson were getting some paperwork done in the First Sgt.'s office (actually all they were doing was signing; Sy did all the work). Lt. Scumbag asked Sgt. Taylor if he was going to carry his field pack or put it in the truck. "We ain't got no truck for this march," Sgt. Taylor said. "No truck, no pack."

"Well, Sergeant, I believe in doing everything the men have to do, so we'll be carrying packs, too." Taylor and Jackson looked at him like he was out of his mind.

"I'm sure that Lt. Nugent would agree with me," Scumbag added, sensing the coming opposition.

First Sgt. Jackson just laughed and handed a paper to Sy to retype because he didn't like the margins. Sgt. Taylor got red in the face though, especially his eagle-shaped nose, which was a sure sign that he was furious.

"Maybe that's what they teach you college kids in ROTC, but in this here Company A, 101st Airborne Division, we do it *our* way — Loo-ten-int."

Now, sergeants are supposed to obey lieutenants and be respectful, but Sgt. Taylor had just spoken with such dripping scorn in his voice that Lt. Scumbag was...well...nonplussed, to say the least. He knew that the sergeant was a Silver Star holder with two combat tours while he, Scumbag, was, militarily speaking, nada. But he didn't know that last part yet. What if he ordered Taylor to carry his own pack and Taylor told him to fuck off? He couldn't take that chance, so he said *he* would carry his pack and the sergeant could do as he pleased.

"Durned right," Sgt. Taylor agreed. "Anything else, Jack?" he asked Jackson.

"Yeah, how about submitting an application for OCS?" (Officers Candidate School)

Sgt. Taylor didn't miss a beat: "Sure, have Abrams type it up and wipe some general's ass with it." He turned and left quick time while Jackson roared laughing, Sy smirked, and Lt. Scumbag looked like a turnip.

Left ... left ... left my wife and forty-nine kids in a starving condition without any gingerbread, thought I did right ... right ... and so on. That's one of the songs we sang while marching through the camp streets. Another one was *Avanti Popolo*, which John Friccero taught us. It was in Italian, so no one except him understood the words. (It was only much later, when John and I were in Military Intelligence in Germany and they kicked him out because of his pinko background in college, that I learned it was from the Communist International. John said he wasn't really a communist, just sang the song to show how ignorant the army was. He was a college professor, for God's sake. When they kicked him

28

out of Intelligence he got a job in Public Information, so he was better off.) The whole company sang, shouted rather, *Avanti Popolo* and John sang the rest of the concert in his beautiful, strong tenor. We only had to know when to come in again with *Avanti Popolo*.

The soldiers from the other companies always came out to watch us march by. We were the coolest company in the regiment, no doubt about it. We also had a real drummer, a black guy whose first name was J.B. They tried to get him to give his real name, but he insisted that was his real name, he had no other, even had a birth certificate to prove it. Most of the other companies' drummers just banged on the drum to the marching beat, but J.B. was a jazz drummer and he made marching a pleasure. We skipped, hopped and dragged. Lt. Scumbag was horrified, but Sgt. Taylor, though he didn't skip or hop, tolerated it looking straight ahead with a small smile. We knew he liked it, although he sure as hell didn't know what *Avanti Popolo* means.

The Night March

We marched out of the camp onto a country road. It was a cold clear night and the sky with the stars pinned to it was so low that you felt you could touch it. Sgt. Taylor gave the walk-easy command. I was alone at the tail end of the four-abreast column walking lightly without a pack and convinced that volunteering was a good idea— sometimes. After a few miles the road narrowed just as the moon came up, giving us the light we would need. Sgt. Silas Taylor had it all figured out, of course. He knew the moon would arrive just when we needed it. He was in the middle and to the left of the column, where he belonged, and Lt. Scumbag bounced along at its head. We compressed ourselves into two columns twice as long from head to ass-end, that is, me.

The road got rougher as we went, but we had already marched it during the day, so we expected that. At about halfway, five miles, the column suddenly stopped and I, dreaming, bumped into the guy in front of me. A couple of minutes later I heard the cry: MEDIC! Shit, that's me. I ran up along the column to where Lt. Scumbag was waving his arms at me. He, Sgt. Taylor and a group of grunts were huddled around someone sitting on the ground. When they opened up for me to pass, I saw it was Fat Boy, I think his name was George something. Apparently, he'd stepped on a rock while going downhill and was holding his ankle and grimacing.

"This man is injured, Medic," Lt. Scumbag said, as though I couldn't see that for myself.

I knelt down alongside him and asked what happened. "My fuckin' ankle, hurts like hell," he whined. Sgt. Taylor knelt beside me and whispered, "Take off his boot."

"Want me to give him a shot of morphine first?" I asked.

"This ain't the movies, Smith. You ain't got no morphine anyway. Just take off his boot and act like you know what you're doing."

"Lay down, Fat Boy. I'm going to take off your boot and see what you got." "Put a blanket under him first," the sergeant said.

I unlaced his boot and pulled it off as gently as I could. You'd think I was amputating the way he squealed. The ankle was red and swollen. I looked in my first-aid kit for the first time and found an elastic bandage. I took it out and looked at Sgt. Taylor, who nodded. So I wrapped it tightly around Fat Boy's ankle.

"Take the extra socks out of his pack and put them on him," Sgt. Taylor said to someone. "And wrap him in another blanket."

"Yes and use a blanket and two rifles to make a stretcher, Lt. Scumbag interjected. "We can carry him that way."

Sgt. Taylor ignored him. "Popeye!" he yelled down the line.

"Yo," came the answer.

"Get yuh ass over here."

Popeye was a skinny little runt, but the only one in the company who could run faster and farther than Sgt. Taylor, if he was motivated, such as by a direct order.

"Run," Taylor told him. "And ah mean run, back to camp, to the hospital, and tell them to send an ambulance here. Tell them it's serious, a man down, or they'll finish their hand of poker before deciding to leave. You come with them, so the dumb bastards don't get lost. Got it?"

"Got it, Sarge." And he took off like Road Runner.

The ambulance arrived in record time. I half expected to see Popeye running along in front of it, leading the way, but he was sleeping on the patient's cot in the back.

"Hell, lieutenant," the young doctor said to Scumbag, "I expected to find a comatose patient, the way your runner described it. This man looks like he sprained his ankle."

"We thought it might be broken, Sir." The doc didn't have any rank on his whites, but Scumbag figured anyone must outrank him. "Of course, the runner, the messenger, is prone to exaggeration, but then sometimes it's better to exaggerate than to ignore a possible serious casualty ..." He would have gone on philosophizing, but the doc turned his back and told his driver to supervise getting Fat Boy into the ambulance. That's when they found Popeye, and unceremoniously tossed him out of the ambulance.

We finished the march, had the day off. Fat Boy came out of the hospital with a cast on his ankle and crutches. No break but some ligaments were strained. Company A won the regimental award for best company the whole four months we were there. They wanted to promote Captain Nugent to major, but he said no, then he'd have to go to regiment and he thought his work as Company Commander was more important at this time of crisis for our country, so they left him alone.

All that's only to give you an idea, a feeling rather, of what

31

infantry basic training was like during the Korean War. Now we come to the really big, the life-changing, maybe even life-saving choice.

The Russian choice

One day a couple of weeks before Basic Training ended, when we had just finished morning roll call, which consisted of Company A's four platoons standing alongside each other and facing Field First Sgt. Taylor, and after all the acting squad leaders had saluted their acting platoon leaders, the acting platoon leaders had about-faced, saluted Sgt. Taylor and yelled, in order: *First Platoon all present and accounted for Sir, Second Platoon ...* and so on, acting Cpl. Sy ran up to me and said that First Sgt. Jackson wants to see me in his office like *now*. I asked Sy what's goin' on, because he knew everything. "Just go, man, it ain't bad news." He said that because when they called you into the office it was usually because someone died at home.

"You Private Frank T. Smith?" the First Sgt. asked me when I stumbled into his office. When I confirmed that I was indeed me, he told me that I was not to go out with the rest of the company on training today. "What are they doing today?"

"Don't know, Sergeant."

"Well, whatever it is you stay here until about oh-eight hundred then go to Classification and Assignment. Be there at oh-eight-thirty."

I stood there with my mouth open.

"That's all, Private."

Before leaving I asked as humbly as I could sound why I was going to Classification & Assignment, whatever that was.

"Don't know, son," Sgt. Jackson said with a lopsided grin.

"Maybe they're gonna classify and assign you, hope it don't hurt. "The Company Clerk will give you a map of Fort Breckinridge and point out where C&A is or is supposed to be."

Maybe I haven't mentioned before that all the buildings in Breckinridge were World-War-Two relics. The barracks had cellars with furnaces, but the smaller buildings, like C&A, used coal-burning pot-bellied stoves. I entered a few minutes early and there were already about a dozen other guys already there, seated, silently, facing a podium. They all looked at me when I entered, saw no stripes on my sleeve, so returned to contemplating the lectern. Finally, at exactly oh-eight-thirty a master-sergeant entered and took his place at the lectern. Although we were a captive audience, we were also a most interested one. I was the only one from Company A. Later in my military career I learned that a master-sergeant at division level is more important and thus more powerful than a colonel, because he actually *does* the work. That may be hyperbole, but it's the impression I had, encouraged by having read James Jones' *From Here to Eternity.*

He took his time contemplating us, his face grim, as if he had a disagreeable tale to tell. Then his face cracked into a grin. "Okay gentlemen, I got some news for you that you're gonna like." He opened a folder and read our names, listed alphabetically. We confirmed that we were us. "All present, good. You guys have been selected to attend the Army Language School in Monterey, California, after basic training for one year ... if you want to of course, you see it's voluntary." No reaction, we were stunned. "You can study a language of your choice," the sergeant went on, "limited to four possibilities. Are you listening?" We were, "Swedish (pause), Russian (pause), Chinese Mandarin (dramatic pause) or Korean."

Any red-blooded American boy would choose Swedish of course, thinking of beautiful blonde Swedish girls whispering sweet nothings into his ear, in Swedish naturally. Except me. I was on a

33

Dostoevsky kick. I don't remember why I started reading *The Brothers Karamazov*, but I did, and it knocked me out. Then Tolstoy. I'd wondered what it must be like to read them in the original, in Russian. Now this guy, this sergeant in camp Breckinridge, Kentucky, was offering me the opportunity to do that, eventually.

"Oh, just one more thing," he said. "There's a catch: if you are accepted to the Army Language School you will have to re-enlist for three years after basic training." He paused for a minute to let that sink in. Draftee time was 18 months whereas three years amounted to 36 months plus the three months of basic training. He stepped down and handed out a paper to each of us. Once back at the lectern he said, "Fill out this form and don't forget to sign it at the bottom."

Under name and serial number (which I still remember by the way: RA51205582) we were to write in our first, second and third language choices. Someone asked if we could think it over and bring the paper back tomorrow. "No, you can't ask your mommy, sonny. You do it now or leave." Everyone, we learned later, put Swedish first, then Russian, Chinese Mandarin and, lastly, Korean — obviously. If I have a guardian angel, he must have been directing my hand as I wrote Russian first, followed by Swedish and Chinese Mandarin. It was an inspired choice!

The sergeant told us we'd be informed when to return. I walked out in a daze which covered my head like a cloud, until I was awakened by some asshole officer who shouted at me to take your hands out of your pockets, soldier, and salute when you see an officer. I took my hands out of my pockets but didn't salute because he'd already passed. But his existence awakened me to the fact that if I was accepted as a student in the Language School it would mean California instead of Korea — at least for a year. I looked around and realized that I had not been walking back to Company A's barracks, but in the opposite direction.

A week later after roll call Acting Cpl. Sy grabbed me again, but this time told me to go directly to Classification and Assignment instead of reporting first to First Sgt. Jackson. Back at C&A the master sergeant took his own miniature roll call: we were all present and accounted for. "OK, listen up. The quota for the Swedish language course had already been filled by the time your applications arrived, so all of you who put Swedish as first choice were rejected. Well, it looks like that means all of you," he grinned, "except — he looked down at the paper in his hand — "Smith. Which one are you?" I raised my hand. "OK, you picked Russian, so you were accepted. You will receive your orders and instructions in due time."

"What about us Sergeant?" a fat guy up front asked.

"Good question Private, shows your interest." I don't know if he was being ironic, but kind of suspect he was. "The Russian course is also full, but you can choose between Chinese Mandarin and Korean." A couple guys got up and left. One of them mumbled: "Swedish, yeah my ass," as he walked out. The sergeant handed out papers again to the future Chinese Mandarin linguists. No one chose Korean. "Smith, you can go." So I did. Later on I thought about my choice of volunteering to be drafted at exactly the right time. If I had waited, the Russian course probably wouldn't have been available, and I'd have wound up in Korea.

Before leaving Basic Training, I must at least mention Agnello. I didn't know him well because he was in a different barracks, but I certainly knew of him, as did we all. After only a few weeks of Basic, he announced that the army was bullshit and he was leaving, which meant deserting. And that was no joke in wartime. He said they turned him down when he applied to be an ambulance driver like Ernest Hemingway. The only thing holding him back was the promise of a week-long leave after eight weeks of Basic, enough time to go home. But the catch — there's always a catch — was if anyone went AWOL the leave was canceled for everyone. Agnello said he'd stay till after the leave before absconding. However, something happened that made Agnello's sacrifice moot. The UN forces in Korea — 90 per cent of which were U.S. — were getting pushed back south of the 38th parallel by the Chinese and North Koreans, so Washington decided to suspend all leaves and get us new guys over there ASAP. The day after the news was given to us Agnello left. We never saw him again. We heard that he went home to Massachusetts where the MPs arrested him.

Neither mustn't I forget Magarino. He was Puerto Rican and our barrack comedian. He pretended to be furious at his superiors for forcing him to shave off his mustache which, according to him, was luxurious and sexy. One afternoon after training he stood in the middle of the barrack and shouted, with his slight Spanish accent, "The sergeant, he tells me *Sound off like you got a pair a balls!* Thank God my wife, she don't hear." He then opened his fly and lifted his testicles plus penis out: "Are not these balls ... or not they are balls?"

On the last day of Basic Training, Company A stood at attention after breakfast: four platoons of 4 squads each totaling about 144 men. The only real cadre present were First Field Sergeant Silas Taylor and First Sergeant Jackson. The Company Commander was absent, probably nursing a hangover. All the rest — squad leaders, assistant squad leaders, platoon leaders — were make-believe, were actors, were us. After the squad leaders reported to the platoon leaders that we were "all present and accounted for, Sir," except Agnello of course, but that was old news, the platoon leaders reported to the Field First Sergeant who reported to the First Sergeant that we were all present and accounted for Sir, First Sgt. Jackson looked behind him and saw in the distance the Company Commander standing as straight as possible. Jackson did a smart about-face and reported: "Company A all present and accounted for, Sir." The C.C. Saluted back, shouted "Carry on, Sergeant," did a left-face and disappeared. Acting Company Clerk

Sy appeared pushing a table on rollers with a pile of papers on top held down by a stone. He stopped next to Sgt. Jackson and read from the first papers, which were our individual orders listed alphabetically.

"Ackerman, Saul G." He handed the orders to Sgt. Jackson. Saul Ackerman — who was killed in Korea I was told — came front and center and Jackson shook his hand, handed him his orders and said "Good luck, son ..." He said the same thing to everyone, but somehow, we felt that he meant it. Most of the Company A trainees were ordered to a transportation unit on the West Coast, which meant being shipped to Japan, finally to infantry units in Korea. The rest were ordered to a transportation unit in New York, which indicated Germany as final destination. They were the lucky ones. But not as lucky as I, whose orders were to report to the Army Language School in Monterey, California, in fifteen days. Another guy who wasn't going overseas right away was Dumbo (I don't remember his real name, but he wasn't called Dumbo only because of his big ears) who volunteered for the newly founded "Special Forces," which was an elite way to die asap. Dumbo volunteered for everything including keeping the coal boilers under the barracks going at night. He was the opposite of Agnello.

Sgt. Silas Taylor was promoted to Master Sergeant, which he certainly deserved. Master Sergeants are respected by their underlings much more than most officers, who are parasites who never work and are provided with room and board free of charge. Generally speaking, if you can stand the bullshit, the army is ideal for the naturally lazy. Except if you're unlucky enough to get involved in a war, like Ackerman did. After my fifteen-day leave, my father drove me to the airport in New York. My duffel-bag didn't fit into the trunk, so we left the trunk-lid open with the bag half out. When we got to the airport the bag wasn't there; it'd either bounced out or was stolen when we stopped for a red light. My father said he'd look for it on the way home, but it was never found.

So I arrived at the Language School with only the clothes on my back. I gradually bought the uniform stuff from quartermaster, but I didn't complain. It was better than Korea.

The Army Language School

The Language School was like a free-of-charge university including room and board. And the food was excellent, way above the normal army fare. We were a Russian class of about eighty students, divided into groups of eight. The teachers were all Russian native speakers, although not necessarily professional educators. But they were all well-educated, at least in Russian. We had class five hours a day, five days a week. With that kind of immersion it would be hard not to learn something, even a lot. Our fun teacher was Romanov, a nephew of Czar Nicholas II, who had been murdered by the Bolsheviks. He was kind of decadent, but had a sense of humor and taught us all the dirty words in Russian, of which there are plenty. His method of correcting pronunciation was by shouting: "There are no cows in Mask-*va!*" (correct pronunciation of "Moscow.")

The Gilded Cage

One night I went to the Gilded Cage in town and was dressed accordingly: blue sports jacket, slacks, loafers without socks, white shirt open to the third button. I arrived early and found a stool at the semi-circular bar, put a fiver on the bar for effect, ordered a Millers High Life, lit a cigarette, and looked around. The bar stools were almost all occupied — by men. Soon they'd be three deep, it being Friday night. The piano was set back in an alcove to the left-rear of the bar. It also had bar stools around it so you could drink there and look at the player with one elbow on the piano. Two young couples were perched on the stools, the men in suits and ties and the giggly women showing a lot of leg. The men were probably asshole officers from Fort Ord, I figured. The piano player was playing *As Time Goes By*, probably requested by one of the girls. That kind of girl always requested that kind of song because they liked to think of themselves as Ingrid Bergman — romantic and teary — without realizing that it wasn't a song you could request, it had to hit you out of the blue. I lit another cigarette and nursed my beer.

The Gilded Cage wasn't really my kind of place, primarily because they only served bottled beer which cost two bits, except for Miller's High Life, which went for thirty cents. Hell, you could get a good glass of draft beer anywhere else for a dime. There were other things I didn't like about it, such as the yellow birdcage

39

hanging over the bar with a live parakeet in it and the bartender wearing a tie and garters on his sleeves. I wondered what it felt like to be a caged bird in that dump. The whole place was like a trinket you could buy in the five-and-ten. And the customers — mostly what you'd call gay today but what we called something else then — thought they were hot shit with their sports jackets and ties and wavy hair and loud laughs. About the only thing good about the Gilded Cage was the piano player, who could play anything you requested. You had to tip him or buy him a drink every time you made a request though, so I never requested anything because I was only a private in the United States Army and my budget didn't include tips, except to waitresses. In fact, I'd only been in the Gilded Cage once before, on a payday, when I wandered in half-drunk without knowing what kind of place it was. Monterey was full of cheap bars and the only reason to go to an expensive one would be on the chance of picking up a girl, which was damn hard in a town that had the Army Language School right up the hill in the Presidium and Fort Ord about three miles away. Monterey wasn't Steinbeck's Cannery Row anymore, and it hadn't yet become a snooty extension of Carmel and Pacific Grove.

"Nice song," a guy said who sidled up next to me. I nodded and looked at him in the mirror. In his thirties I guessed, suntanned, casually well dressed. He was smiling at my profile. "And from a nice picture," I agreed.

"Saw it three times myself," the guy said. "You?"

"About the same."

"You want your drink here, Jacky?" the bartender asked the guy.

"Yes, thank you, Sal."

The bartender went to the end of the bar and came back with a glass with an inch of whiskey and soda in it. He put a coaster in front of Jacky and placed the drink on it.

EXILE'S END — A MEMOIR

"That was hardly worth the trip, Sal," Jacky said, grinning.

Sal grinned back and went off to tend a customer. I drank down my beer, knowing I wouldn't have to nurse it any longer. Jacky drank his down too. "Let me buy you a drink. Wouldn't you prefer scotch?"

"No, I'll stick with Millers thanks." A subtle answer, so Jacky wouldn't get the right idea.

"Suit yourself," he said. "Sal, another scotch for me and a Millers for ... What did you say your name was?"

"Frank."

"For Frank," Jacky said smoothly, more to me than to the bartender, who had moved on anyway.

"Thanks."

"Cigarette?" He held a pack of filter-tipped Parliaments, though my Marlboro's were plainly visible on the bar. What the hell, I thought, why waste them? and took a Parliament. Jacky's gold-plated lighter flicked open under my nose so I didn't even have to lean forward to reach the tiny flame. I dragged and could hardly taste the smoke, because of the dammed filter-tip.

"Thanks."

"Are you from around here, Frank?"

"No, New York." Actually Brooklyn, but that always caused a laugh or some wiseguy remark, so I had learned to say New York instead. Hell, most people west of New Jersey didn't even know that Brooklyn is in New York City.

"You don't sound like you're from New York."

One thing good about learning a foreign language is that you have to concentrate on your pronunciation, and I had begun to watch my English to weed out the Brooklynese.

"Well, I am."

"In the army here?"

"Yeah."

"Ford Ord?"

"Language School."

"Thank God!"

I looked at him. "Why?"

"Well, you know," Jacky said smiling, "you can at least have an intelligent conversation with a Language School student, which isn't often the case with the ones from Fort Ord. You're an officer, I suppose."

"Why do you suppose that? Officers are assholes."

He laughed loudly. "Frank, you're a man after my own heart, and you're absolutely right. Officers are assholes."

I glanced at the couples at the piano, but they obviously couldn't hear. "So why did you suppose I was one?"

"Oh god, please don't be angry. I just wanted to know, and I couldn't very well have said: You're a private, I suppose? I mean what if you were an officer. Where would I be then?"

"Up shit's creek?" I laughed as I said it.

"Absolutely."

"Not many officers in the Language School," I said. I liked the game of denigrating officers but kept my voice low. "They're too dumb."

"I agree, absolutely, at least the few I've met."

I didn't say anything. I was waiting for the proposition.

"What language are you studying?" Jacky asked.

"Russian."

"Russian? Wow, that must be difficult."

"Yeah, but it's better than Korean or Chinese."

"Oh God, yes. I speak some French myself, but I'd never think of trying a difficult language like Russian. Whatever made you pick it?"

"I didn't have much choice. They called a few of us to Classification and Assignment one day in Basic Training and said that the tests showed we had linguistic abilities and offered a choice between Swedish, Russian, Korean and Chinese Mandarin, we should write down our preference. I put Russian because I'd like to be able to read Dostoevsky and Tolstoy in the original. So I got it — Russian I mean. The others all put down Swedish and none of them got anything. They're in Korea now."

"I love Dostoevsky," Jacky crooned.

"Yeah, well I'm still far away from being able to read him in Russian, the way the course is going, prisoner interrogation exercises, that kind of shit."

"How long have you been here?"

"Two months."

"So, you have ten months left?"

So, Jacky knew that Russian was a year-long course. Well, why not? He was from around here.

"That's right."

"Wonderful!" He patted the back of my hand. "We have time to get acquainted."

"Here it comes," I thought. "Yeah, but I doubt if there's time to learn enough Russian to read Dostoevsky or Tolstoy in the original. They're tough."

"Would you be very disappointed if you couldn't, Frank?"

"Not very, but disappointed, sure, I guess."

"I think it's a question of what one expects from life. If one has no expectations, one can't be disappointed. Don't you think so?"

"Well, I think life would be pretty boring without expectations."

"But not disappointing."

"I don't know about that."

"Have you ever been disappointed, Frank," Jacky asked and laughed. "I don't know where you find room for all that beer. Sal, another round, please."

"You're keeping up with me."

"Yes, but there's less liquid involved."

"More potent liquid though...and yes, I have."

"Have what, Frank?"

"Yes, I have been disappointed."

"But you're so young to have been disappointed, unless in love." He smiled. Actually, he was a handsome guy. "But then Romeo was awfully young. Have you been disappointed in love then, Frank? I have, often."

"Yeah, especially the last time," I said, wondering why I was about to tell him about Olga when I hadn't mentioned her to anyone else, not even my buddies up at the Presidium. I was too young to know that we are always on the lookout for a sympathetic listener. And Jacky was certainly one, while my buddies would only have shaken their heads and laughed.

"Oh, do tell me." Jacky leaned to his left until our shoulders were touching and looked at me intently, ready to listen.

"Well, I went up to San Francisco ..." I didn't mention that it had

44

been last weekend. I had driven up alone in my 1949 Hudson Hornet the Friday after payday, alone because I'm a loner, that's what people said about me and I suppose it was true. I had only one real friend on the hill in the Language School, Jim McCrea, but Jim was Black (called "Negro" back then) which was a big disadvantage when girls were involved. In fact, it was a disadvantage when anything was involved once you got off base. There was no Jim Crow in California like in the South, but there was a more subtle discrimination. Jim and I had driven around sightseeing and had eaten together in restaurants and went to Shorty's bar, which was just outside the base, at least once a week to drink ten cent beer and listen to jazz on the jukebox they had there and talk a lot. But whenever there were likely looking girls in the place, which wasn't often, I regretted being with Jim because it was impossible to pick up a couple of white girls — and they were always white and always in pairs — if you were with Jim. Even if you went to town you might get into trouble if some townie or redneck from Fort Ord decided to pick a fight because Jim was black. Jim knew it, of course, so he never went to the bars in town. It was a rotten situation that I hated, but if you were after pussy that was how it was and if I had to choose between pussy — or the chance of it — and Jim ... well, that's the way it was.

It took about three hours to get to Frisco because there was no good thruway yet. Once there I checked into the YMCA for three bucks a night that I paid in advance and went cruising. I had consumed a lot of beer by the time I walked into that bar without noticing its name — an oversight I would eternally regret.

It was about midnight and the place was jumping. There was a rectangular bar, served by bartenders on all four sides, a crowded dance floor and booths. The first unusual thing was that there was a dance floor at all, the second that the place was well lighted instead of half-dark. It was the antithesis of the Gilded Cage. I stood at the bar and ordered a Bud draft. The booths ran all along the walls and I inspected them. There were a lot of girls in the place, but they were already with guys. I regretted that I hadn't found the place sooner. Now I'd have to try to cut someone out or wait for someone new to come in.

Then I spotted Olga. Although there must have been a lot of servicemen there — we were in the middle of the Korean War after all — none were in uniform except the sailor in a funny uniform who was sitting in the booth across from her. The sailor moved his hand brusquely and knocked over a wine bottle. The girl tried to wipe the spilled wine with a paper napkin while he laughed. He must have been drunk. I saw my opportunity and grabbed a rag from the sink below the bar and walked over to them. "You won't get it dry with that piece of paper, Miss," I said, and wiped up the beer. The sailor clapped me on the shoulder laughing and said something in French.

"What'd he say?" I asked her.

"He thinks you're a waiter. He asked for another bottle of wine." She smiled at me, and I smiled back. She had an accent which I recognized, having heard it often enough during the past two months.

"He looks like he's had enough," I said. "But hey, I'm not a waiter, so don't ask me."

The Frenchy suddenly keeled over on his side.

"What'd I tell you?" I pushed him upright and sat down next to him across from the girl and the sailor slumped against me. "You're Russian, aren't you?"

"Does it show so much?"

I looked her over carefully as if to decide whether it showed. Her cheekbones were a little high, eyes set wide apart, full lips. Her brown hair flowed over her shoulders front and back with ragged bangs on her forehead. She was wearing a greenish print dress that

46

looked like it came straight out of a World War II Care package. Her bosom was full, apparent although the dress was buttoned up almost to her neck to anyone who looked, and I was looking. No makeup. Pretty. She looked very young at first glance, but her eyes were older.

"No," I said, "I recognize the accent."

"Most people think I'm Polish. How did you guess I'm Russian?"

"That's because there's so many Poles around and not many Russians," I said. "I recognized the accent because I'm around Russians all the time. I'm studying Russian at the Army Language School. *Ya izuchayu russkie Yazuik f'armeskiye shkole Yizikom.*"

At that she clapped her hands happily and let out a stream of Russian of which I only caught a few words.

"Hey, wait a minute, I've only been at it a couple of months." She repeated it slowly and, though I still didn't understand everything, I got the drift: "How wonderful. The only people I know here who speak Russian are Russians, and they bore me."

"Do I bore you?"

"Of course not. That's what I meant." We both smiled. The juke box started to play *As Time Goes By* and I tried to think of the word for dance in Russian and finally decided that I never knew it.

"Would you like to dance?"

"*Konyechno.*"

I pushed the sailor away until he was leaning against the wall, but not until after his head bounced against it.

"Be careful!" she cried.

"Don't worry," I said as we walked to the dance floor, "he can feel no pain. "Where did you ever find that guy?"

"He's a friend of my uncle who lives in Paris. Actually, he's the son of my uncle's friend." She looked back at the sailor. "His ship sails at dawn and he has to get back somehow."

We began a bit stiffly, but she was soon snuggling up against me and I could smell the delicate perfume of her hair. I pulled my crotch back so she wouldn't feel my incipient erection, not yet anyway.

"*Kak vasho imyo*?" I asked, the easiest question there was.

She laughed though.

"What's so funny?"

"You're so formal. My name is Olga, but you would normally use the familiar form of the pronoun under the present circumstances: *Kak tvayo imyo*?"

"We haven't had the familiar form yet."

"Well, we can't very well continue as if I were your professor, so we better speak English."

"Excellent idea, Olga. I love your name."

"Oh dear, and it's such a common name in Russia."

"Not here. Here it's beautiful — to me at least."

"And your name?" she asked leaning back to look in my eyes, which caused her hips to swivel into me.

"Frank." My erection was in full bloom. I moved back so it was only touching her lightly.

"You don't have to do that," she said. "I like it."

Godamm, my dream had been answered, my ship had come in. I was on the verge of shacking up in Frisco with a beautiful Russian woman, who not only liked hard-ons and wasn't afraid to say so, but could help me learn Russian.

A Chubby Checker teenybop number blasted out of the jukebox and Olga said she didn't like it so we went to the bar instead of back to the booth, where Frenchy was still out cold. She didn't want anything more to drink though, said she already had too much wine. I ordered a beer, drank it down and ordered another. I had worked up a real thirst from dancing and the expectation of what was to come — that night and many future weekends.

Olga took a sip of my beer. "I don't think that Philippe is in any condition to get back to his ship," she said, frowning.

"He's only asleep," I said. "He'll be all right."

"I hope so." She looked at her watch. "It's almost two o'clock."

"Good. This place will be open another hour. Let's dance." The divine Sarah Vaughan was singing *A Foggy Day*. She meant in London town, but San Francisco town was pretty foggy too.

"I don't know how he'll get back to his ship."

"After this number we'll go back, wake him up and put him in a cab," I said, hoping that either the sailor or she had money to pay for it.

"Oh no, we couldn't do that."

"He's probably got money, sailors always do after hoarding it up at sea."

"That's just it," she protested. "You know what taxi drivers are like. A drunk sailor. He'd be robbed ..."

"Rolled," I corrected her. "Not necessarily. All cabbies aren't crooks. Why are you worrying about him so much anyway?" I didn't want to sound jealous, but I was.

"Don't you see? I'm responsible for him. They gave him my name in Paris because they knew he was coming here. He called me — he's very nice when he's sober — and I took him out to see San Francisco. He had too much to drink. If anything happens to him, I'd be responsible. Do you see?"

"Yeah, I guess so."

"You have a car, Frank. Could you take him?"

"Well, I don't know," though I did know: I couldn't refuse her. "Where's his ship at?"

He said it was at l'ille du tresor. Was it a joke?"

"No, that would be Treasure Island, it's a naval base under the Bay Bridge to Oakland."

"So you know it!"

"I passed it a couple of times going over the bridge, that's all. I saw the sign."

"Will you take him, Frank, please?"

"OK., we'll all go." I tried to push her into dance mode again, but she stood still.

"No, I'm a foreigner, they wouldn't let me in. And ... well ... my papers aren't completely in order yet."

Shit. Was she a spy? Were they both spies? Who cares. "But you're in the military. They'd let you in. I'll wait here for you."

"What if this place is closed when I get back? You can't stand waiting on the corner at three o'clock in the morning."

Her eyes opened wide; they were green like her dress. "I'll give you my telephone number. If it's closed when you get back, call me." She smiled. "I'll be waiting."

My first priority had been to go to her place when the bar closed. Failing that, I wanted her phone number. I wasn't sure that she'd give it to me. After all, I was only a barroom pick up. Now, however, I was sure of getting it, and I couldn't refuse her anyway. "Okay," I said, "let's get it over with."

We went back to the booth, and I shook Frenchy and slapped

his cheeks. He woke up and babbled in French.

Olga took one of the paper napkins from its holder and wrote her telephone number on it. I put it in my pocket, I couldn't remember which one afterwards, although I certainly thought about it a lot.

"C'mon Robespierre, let's get you presentable." I pulled him across the booth seat and got him standing.

"What are you doing?" Olga asked.

"Taking him to the john to put some cold water on his face and get him to take a leak or he'll piss all over the car."

"Jesus, I never saw anyone so drunk from wine," I said as we maneuvered him out of the bar upon our return from the men's room. "Refused to piss, that's his problem."

"He was a little tipsy when he came to my place," Olga said, sounding as though she was defending him. "Who knows how much he had to drink."

My car was a block away and as the three of us weaved downhill the sailor started singing — in French of course.

"Christ, just what I needed," I said. "Tell him to shut up before the MPs hear him, or SPs if that'll impress him more."

He shut up quick when Olga translated. We dumped him in the front seat of the Hudson and Olga kissed me on the lips, not passionately, but lovingly yes, I decided.

I took some wrong turns, so it took longer to find the Bay Bridge than I'd expected. The fog had gotten worse, so I had to drive more carefully than usual. I remembered that the sign to Treasure Island was somewhere near the middle of the bridge, so I hugged the right lane in order not to miss the turn-off, which was on the bridge itself. The fog was even thicker on the bridge, and I drove slowly, hunched over the steering wheel. Then I felt the car descending and had a sinking feeling in my stomach. I had missed the exit to Treasure Island. And I couldn't very well make a U-turn on a bridge when I couldn't see what might be coming from the other direction. So, I had to continue into Oakland, turn and go back over the bridge. I knew there was only one turn-off, and it was on the right side going towards Oakland. So, I had to drive all the way back into Frisco, turn and head back to Oakland.

This time I went ten miles an hour and finally saw the sign: it was hanging over the middle of the bridge, that's why I hadn't seen it the first time across. They must have moved it. I cursed and eased the Hudson down the ramp onto Treasure Island and stopped at the guard booth.

"Where ya goin', sir," a huge SP said. The "sir" was just in case I was an officer.

"I'm trying to get this French sailor back to his ship," I said, trying to sound like one.

"Uh huh. ID, please."

I showed him my ID, which definitely established my non-officer status.

"Where ya stationed, soldier?" the SP asked.

"Army Language School, Monterey."

"What's the matter with ya friend?"

I looked over at the sailor, who had fallen asleep again. "He had one too many, I guess." I gave him a jab in the chest with my elbow to wake him up. "He's French."

"Yeah, I had a bunch of 'em rollin' in tonight. What about you?"

"No sweat, I'm okay."

"You better be. I keep your ID and you can pick it up when you leave." He noted down the Hudson's license plate number on a chart and went back into his booth.

"Hey," I yelled, "can you tell me where the French ship is?"

The SP checked a chart hanging in the booth and said: "Pier 21. Go straight till ya can't no more, turn right till ya can't no more, then right again and that's it. Got a French flag on it I guess."

"What's a French flag look like?"

"How the fuck should I know."

I followed the SP's instructions and found the ship. An armed French sailor on guard duty was standing at the foot of the gangplank. I looked at my watch: three o'clock. Shit, the bar was closing. What's it called? "Hey, Frenchy," I said to the sailor, "what's the name of that bar we were in?"

He looked at me blankly.

"Comment lapel le bar?" No reaction.

"Hey," I called to the guard, "come and get this asshole." He didn't move. I got out, opened the door and dragged Frenchy out. Then I grabbed the hat with the red pompon from the seat and placed it on his head and pushed him at the sailor, who had no choice but to catch him.

"Adieu, shitheads."

I parked on a deserted street in San Francisco and looked through my pockets for the napkin. It wasn't there. I looked desperately, turning my pockets out. Then I took a flashlight from the glove compartment and searched the car — floor, seats, everywhere. No napkin.

"Can we help you, sir?" one of the two MPs who appeared behind me said.

"No, I was just looking for sumpin." Damn it, I wasn't drunk anymore, why was I slurring my speech.

"You in the service?"

"Yeah. Who isn't?" Wise guys answers, just what MPs like to hear.

"Let's see your ID."

Here we go again.

Finally, they let me go but made me leave my car where it was, claiming I was drunk, and told me to go right back to the Y and if they saw me again that night, I'd spend the rest of it in the clink.

All day and most of the night Sunday I searched for the bar where I had found and lost Olga but didn't find it. It was as if it had vanished into thin air or never really existed. At five o'clock in the morning I drove back to Monterey. I had to be in class at eight and sick calls on Monday mornings were frowned upon.

"Frank," Jacky said with a crooked smile, "I can imagine how you felt—and I'm sorry, truly I am."

My glass was empty, and I called Sal without bothering to wait for Jacky to invite me to have another.

"On the other hand, I think it goes to prove my thesis."

"Oh yeah? How's that?"

"Well, if you hadn't had the expectation that you'd found the perfect shack job who would help you with Russian as well, you wouldn't have been disappointed when she didn't materialize. See what I mean?"

"Yeah, I guess so." But it was more than that. I had fallen head over heels in love with Olga and I needed to find her. No need to tell Jackie that though.

As Time Goes By was being played again.

"God, I'm beginning to hate that song," Jacky said.

"Me too." I hadn't mentioned the detail that that was the song Olga and I had first danced to.

"What kind of music do you like, Frank, I mean really like?"

"Oh, you know, Jazz, blues. Sarah Vaughan knocks me out, but I guess she's not coming in here."

"My God, Frank, I knew we were kindred spirits," Jacky gushed. "Listen, I have an idea."

Here it comes, finally.

"Let's go to my place. I have the most fantastic jazz collection you ever heard, including plenty of Sarah Vaughan, before she went commercial."

"I like her commercial too."

"Well so do I, but the non-commercial stuff is better, believe me. How about it?"

"Sounds good. Where do you live?"

"Carmel." Exactly where I had guessed he lived.

"Oh, no then, I couldn't go there."

"Why in heaven's name not?"

"No gas."

Jacky laughed, obviously much relieved. "No problem my dear friend, we'll go in my car and I'll bring you back later, if you like, or tomorrow. I have plenty of room."

"Naw, I always like to have my own wheels," I intoned, smoking calmly. "Thanks anyway."

Jacky laughed again. "Frank, you're amazing. You make problems out of nothing. Come on, let's get gas for your car, silly."

"I'm afraid I'm sort of broke, Jacky," I said, although there were still four dollars and seventy cents in front of me on the bar.

"I had no intention of letting you pay for it even if you had the money. When you're my guest it means in everything." He clapped me on the shoulder. "Sal, my bill, please!"

I only needed about a dollar's worth of gas to get to Carmel and back, but I told the attendant at the service station to fill it up. I looked at my watch: ten o'clock, plenty of time. Jacky had pulled his white Mercedes into the station away from the pumps and stood waiting with his arms folded and a big grin on his face. When the attendant hung up the gas hose he strolled over and paid for my gas.

"Follow me, okay Frank? Can't lose that car." He put his wallet in his pocket and started back to his Mercedes whistling *As Time Goes By*, realized it and stopped.

"Jacky," I called.

"Yes, Frank?" He turned around and came back. "What is it?"

"I'm not going to your place, Jacky. I needed the gas to get to Frisco, see? To look for Olga."

Jacky was openly crestfallen, but he didn't beg, I have to give him that. "I see," he said, looking at the ground. Actually, I felt sorry for him. He was a nice guy, basically — but he wasn't Olga.

I got back into the Hudson, closed the door and said through the open window as I started the engine: "You shouldn't have expectations, Jacky, and you wouldn't be disappointed." I didn't mean it sarcastically, although it came out that way.

I closed the window against the cold drizzle, turned on the windshield wipers and gunned the Hudson Hornet towards San Francisco where I, at least, still had expectations. However, you'll be disappointed (or relieved, she could have been a spy) that I never found Olga, not even the bar. Nevertheless, it was true!

I should explain something about all that. First, I didn't tell Jacky the whole story, just the basics. That was enough for him. You may wonder how I could remember it in such detail when it was so long ago. Well, perhaps the details aren't that exact, especially the dialogues. But basically, essentially, it's true.

Once, probably before the Olga incident, I was in a bar in downtown Monterey on a weekday evening, so there were no soldiers from Fort Ord, who could only get weekend passes. I had already been browsing, drinking cheap beer, so I was feeling no pain, as they say. The bar wasn't in the same class as the Gilded Cage. Actually, It was a dump. There were only a few people in it, three or four young men, obviously townies, and a pretty girl. I gave her the eye, she gave it back accompanied by a silent smile. This went on until one of the townies noticed my interest. I must explain that townies hated soldiers, don't know why, maybe because soldiers were the horniest toads around and openly chased their girls. The soldiers from Fort Ord, knew this, and usually hunted in pairs or threes.

The girl slid off her bar stool and came in my direction. She walked the length of the bar but passed me and stood before the cigarette machine behind me. She put some coins in and, while it noisily digested them, whispered to me: "You better get outta here — quick." Clearly a warning. And she sashayed back down the bar. It was almost three o'clock in the morning when the bar would close and if I waited, we'd all be leaving together and the way those townies were glaring at me I didn't think it was a good idea. So, I picked up my change from the bar and casually opened and walked out the door. As I was closing the door after me, I saw the three guys get off their stools and head toward the exit. The street was deserted, so I took off running and the three guys took off after me. I crossed the street and turned the corner toward where my car was parked. It was about twenty yards down the street, and I knew I'd never be able to reach it, open the locked door with my key, get in and start the motor, which was real lazy starting, and drive off before they caught me.

I was passing an alleyway and turned into it hoping to be able to hide. But it turned out to be a courtyard with no exit. A perfect place to get beaten up. To the right I noticed a line of three of four garbage cans near but not quite against the wall. I slipped behind them and sat down on the ground. Luckily it was very dark. I heard a voice from the street yell, "Hey, he might have gone in here." One or more came into the courtyard, I could hear them breathing out of breath, I stopped breathing. "Nah, he ain't here, musta run like hell." "Yeah, let's go back before the joint closes and get another beer." They left. I stayed put just in case. The next thing I knew the sun was reflecting off the garbage cans, I had fallen asleep, it was morning. I stood up aching all over and walked out of the alley. My car — that old Hudson Hornet — was parked close. I got in and drove back up to the Presidium and fell into bed. It was Sunday.

The two guys I was most friendly with in my barracks were my next-door cubicle neighbors, so to speak: Fred and Junior, students of Korean. Junior was Fred's Sancho Panza, I was merely a neighbor. Fred was from Reno, Nevada, where not only gambling was legal, but also prostitution. Fred invited us to drive up to Reno — in my car — one weekend essentially to visit a bordello, a.k.a whorehouse. It was a dump on the outskirts of Reno. The madam welcomed us. We paid in advance, I forget how much, but it was certainly cheap. She told us to sit down and had a very short (3) parade of "girls" march in for selection. It was like an animal fair. Fred, experienced as he was, quickly selected the prettiest (or least homely) of the three and was led by her into one of the interior rooms; same with Junior, who selected the second least homely, thereby leaving me with the least pretty or most homely. She led me into a small room containing a chair and a bed. She sat on the bed and told me with a sergeant-like authority, to stand in front of her and lower my pants and underpants. I obeyed and she squeezed my limp penis to test for venereal disease. After I passed the test, she said: "How dya want it?" I was shocked and disgusted at how demeaning the process was — more to her than to me. "I don't," I said and left the room. Back in the reception area I sat down to wait for Fred and Junior. The Madam didn't seem surprised to see me back so soon and said nothing.

Fred directed us to a hotel cum gambling den where we got cheap but decent rooms paid for by Fred. This was his invitation. The hotels in Reno figured correctly that they would earn much more from the guests' gambling losses. But this trip to Reno is not the reason for mentioning Fred and Junior here. The reason is that I had an inexplicably strong desire to visit Mexico. It was possible to drive to San Francisco or Reno on a Friday afternoon and return on Sunday, but Mexico was too far. Therefore, I insisted that we three — Fred. Junior and I — meet on the steps of the City Hall of Mexico City on New Years Day when we would surely no longer be in the army and would be able to afford such a rendezvous. I made them swear that they would. Of course, we all forgot about it once leaving Monterey behind us. I mention it now because it seems related to the many years I subsequently spent in Argentina and my relation to other South American countries as well as to Spain. As though I subconsciously knew it all in advance.

The Long Drive Home

At the end of the Russian course, we had thirty days leave before shipping overseas according to the language we had studied: Europeans (German, Russian, Serbo-Croatian, etc.) from New York to Germany; Asiatics (Chinese, Korean, Japanese, etc.) from San Francisco to Tokyo — for further assignment. Spanish wasn't taught; I guess we had more than enough Spanish speakers at home. We received travel expenses to home, New York for me. The expenses were calculated according to distance, so we could either use the money to buy an airline ticket, for example, or drive by car, if you had one, and save the money. Someone — I'll call him Sgt. Krankenhauser because I forget his name — put a notice on the bulletin board that he was driving to New York and could take two passengers to share gas costs and driving time. I jumped at it. Sgt. Krankenhauser said okay, he was leaving in two days, did I know anyone else. I was the only one who answered. I told Jim McCrea, who said sure, he could take a bus or train for the short trip from New York to Washington. We intended to drive the northern route across the United States. But on the day before we were to leave a tremendous snowstorm hit most of the northern U.S. making it impossible to drive across safely for at least a week. Sgt. Krankenhauser said that he had intended to go via the north because the highways are better, but since that is no longer possible, we can go via the southern route. He realized that this could be problematic due to Jim's color, but if we all drove, we could drive right across without stopping. I was fine with that because I had no idea what it meant. Jim was unsure, but finally agreed, thereby showing his confidence in us.

We had to stop outside Phoenix to fix a tire. While Sgt. Krankenhauser waited while the tire was being fixed, Jim and I went into a bar. We were the only customers. I said to the bartender: "Two beers, please." He replied, without looking at us, "We don't serve colored people here." I was shocked. My God, I thought, and this is Arizona, cowboys and Indians, not the deep south. We walked out and back to the car.

The idea of all three driving, without stopping to sleep in a bed is one thing and the reality is another thing. While only one is driving, it doesn't necessarily mean that the other two are sleeping sitting up. Our first stop was in New Mexico in a nice looking "Motel for Negro Travelers." It was on the highway, that is, not in a city. We asked if all three of us could stay there for one night. The manager-owner, a Black lady said of course we could. The next morning at breakfast she asked if we intended traveling together farther into the South. We told her we were going to the east coast. She told us we would really need the "Negro Traveler's Green Book." She handed me the book, a magazine really, with a list of all the hotels, motels and private homes, where Negros could stay overnight. Remember, this was 1952, before Martin Luther King was even known, and the South was totally segregated. The movement for racial justice still had a decade to go.

We thanked the lady and drove on and on. When we stopped to eat, Jim stayed in the car while Sgt. Krankenhauser and I entered the restaurant and ordered three meals with drinks to go, and we ate together in the car. Even the toilets and drinking fountains were segregated. "For white," and "For colored." I had heard or read about such things but experiencing them is different and much stronger. And what was Jim feeling? He didn't say anything, nor did we. What could we say? It's just the way it was.

The next place we stopped was Jackson, Mississippi, of all places. You couldn't get any deeper into the deep south. There were only two addresses in the Green Book. It was late at night, and we were exhausted, although Sgt. Krankenhauser did most of the driving. He didn't really like others driving his precious car, although I doubt it would have made any difference if he did. You can't really sleep sitting up at 75 miles an hour. We seemed to be on the main drag. After a few blocks we came to an all-night diner. We can ask here, Krankenhauser said. "Why don't you go in and ask, Smitty?" So, I went in. There were a few men at the counter, eating or drinking coffee or beer, and a few more seated in booths. And a counterman, also the cook I supposed. Country music coming from a jukebox. A bell tinkled when I entered and closed the door. Everyone stopped talking, turned to look at me, then turned back to whatever they were doing.

"Yes sah, what can I do for you? Don't have much left this time a night. Ham or bacon and eggs anyway you want 'em"

"No thanks. Can you please tell me where Lee Street is?"

His welcoming smile dropped away. He called out to the rest: "Lee Street, that's in nigger town, ain't it?"

"Yeah," a guy said from a booth. "That your car out there?" He pointed with his thumb out a window at the only car with lights on.

"Yes, can you tell me how to get to Lee Street?" My Yankee accent sounded like guilt. They were all watching me now.

"Straight ahead to the traffic light, turn right two blocks, and that's it."

"Thanks." I hurried out before he could ask why I wanted to go to a street in nigger town.

"Straight ahead to the traffic light, then right two blocks." I said to Krankenhauser trying to sound calm, which I wasn't.

"How far is it to the traffic light?" Krankenhauser asked in his German accent.

"I don't know, just go please." He looked at me, understood and went.

Through deserted streets and after turning right at the traffic light we drove two blocks and were suddenly in the Negro section, poor with ramshackle houses and broken sidewalks and potholed streets. At least there was some life though. The first address in the Green Book was a dilapidated, dirty-looking two-story house with the upstairs windows without glass. We drove on. The second place looked better, even had a sign hanging on the front porch reading "Hotel rest-a-body." We stopped and Jim went in. He came out and said it was okay, gave me his wallet, said he'd paid in advance. I said we'd pick him up in the morning early. Sgt. Krankenhauser and I drove back out of town to a roadside motel he'd spotted on the way in. Swimming pool and all. I felt like crying from shame. The next morning after breakfast we brought a plastic cup of coffee and a couple of croissants with us for Jim. He was sitting on the steps of the porch of the hotel when we drove up. I gave him back his wallet. He said he'd already had breakfast, which was pretty good, but he'd take what we brought anyway.

The next overnight was in Macon, Georgia. The Negro neighborhood was much better than the one in Jackson, what we saw of it at least. There were several hotels. Jim picked one and we went through the same procedure — like veterans.

The next evening, we finally got to Washington DC, where we dropped Jim off. I don't remember the rest of the trip to New York or exactly where Sgt. Krankenhauser left me.

The thirty-day leave in my Brooklyn neighborhood is also mostly a blur, except for the tearfully dramatic scene of Dottie's (my girlfriend after Patricia) and my final break-up. Her mistake was to offer to wait for me after climax rather than before. And the softball game in the vacant lot across from the Holy Innocents Church, where I hit a ground-rule double off the garage roof in the outfield, which won the game. We had all donated a dime (the price of a glass of draft beer at Clancy's across the street) to the pot, so my team drank our beer free financed by the losing team. It was great fun with no hard feelings.

Germany

All I remember about the crossing to Germany in a so-called "Liberty ship," a World War Two relic that bounced over the North Atlantic Ocean like a cork for two weeks, is us grunts piled below sea-level miserably seasick. I'd rather not think about it.

In the port city of Bremerhaven, I found myself again in a Classification and Assignment office. But this time it was a huge hall where the whole boatload of us grunts had to be classified and assigned. So, it took a while to get to the desk of a corporal who stuck out his hand without looking at me. I handed him my orders. He wrote in the name of an infantry unit somewhere in Germany and handed it back still without looking at me and called for the next guy.

I saw Jim McCrea in the coffee shop. We'd arrived in the same tub called a ship. We compared orders to see if we'd been assigned to the same unit. The answer was no, Jim had been assigned to a military intelligence unit and I to the infantry. He said that couldn't be, that because of our Russian language training we should both be in military intelligence; if he was then I should also be. He said I should go back to that unseeing corporal and tell him he made a mistake — but I shouldn't mention Jim, in case the mistake was his assignment. He said that wouldn't surprise him, being Black that is.

So, I went back and jumped the line and handed the corporal my original orders and the one he had given me and said, "Looks like there's a mistake here Corporal, I graduated from the Army Language School so I should be in an M.I. unit." I spoke as if I knew what I was talking about when all I really knew was what Jim told me. The corporal looked up at me for the first and only time. Then he sighed and crumpled up the orders he had given me and threw it into his overflowing wastepaper basket. He took another form paper, wrote the name of an M.I. Unit in Frankfurt on it and handed it back without looking at me and called for the next guy. I didn't even have time to say thank you, which I wouldn't have done anyway.

Jim McCrea's military intelligence unit was responsible for delivering "confidential supplies" (cigarettes and whiskey for spies) from Frankfurt to Berlin. Jim drove a truck once a week to Berlin over the one road allowed by the Russians through East Germany. He stayed over a few days enjoying Berlin, where most of the girls didn't care what color he was, then headed back to Frankfurt to start over again. "Best job in the army," he said, smiling broadly.

64

Going back to the corporal like that was absolutely necessary for my future, as you will soon see, but it wasn't a true choice of my own. I was only doing what Jim told me to do. But what the hell, "a choice is a choice."

Frankfurt

I was first sent to the Gutleut Kaserne — a huge German Wehrmacht fortress a block or two from the main train station — doing nothing except walking around Frankfurt with no money to speak of, until one day the Master Sergeant told me to get a car in the motor pool and drive to the airport wearing civilian clothes. He interrupted himself to ask me if I knew where the airport is. I said sure, which was true as I had passed it several times on the autobahn leading to and from Frankfurt. I was to pick up two "sources" — our word for spies — a German couple, Herr und Frau Goebels, on the 9 P.M. flight from Berlin. Frau Goebels would be carrying a copy of the news magazine "Der Spiegel" in her left hand. I thought it kind of strange that I was driving a military *Opel* car wearing civilian clothes. But it was just one of many dumb contradictions I was to experience in the future. I drove to the airport and saw that TWA had flights from Berlin at 9 and 10 P.M. The sources didn't arrive on the 9 o'clock flight so I waited for the 10 o'clock flight which they weren't on either, so I called the sergeant and told him they hadn't arrived, what should I do? "Come back," he growled. "They're here, they took a taxi."

I guess I hadn't made a very good impression. I found out later that the Frankfurt airport has two sides, one civilian, where I was, and one military, where I was not. So, the two sources had of course arrived on the military flight at 9 P.M. Well, how was I to know if nobody told me? I asked myself. I was then sent to Oberammergau in Bavaria to attend two weeks of spy training at the Army Intelligence and Military Police School. (It's where I found out about the airport.) Most memorable was a weekend bus trip to Venice organized by the USO and guided by two pretty and pleasant American young ladies.

But something else happened, which may have had an effect on my future. As part of my training, after *How To Follow someone and not be followed by anyone*, I was sent by myself to a town a few miles outside Munich, and then another town farther away. I was to find out about a bridge in the first town and foreigners in the second. I was given bus fare and a Minox camera, a gadget about the size of a pack of cigarettes, in fact disguised as one. The problem was that I spoke no German. I found the bridge all right. But so what! I crossed it, crawled down through the underbrush on the other side and snapped a few pictures. Of course, I could have taken the pictures in the open without getting dirty and scratched, but I figured that could be suspicious. I'd seen too many movies.

I took the bus again to the next town where I entered into a *Gasthaus* and sat at the bar next to a friendly looking guy. I ordered *ein Bier, bitte* in an accent that identified me at once as an American.

"You American?" the guy asked. He was red-cheeked, pot-bellied and obviously spent too much time in bars.

"Yes. You?"

He laughed: "German, from ass to elbow. But I been in da States."

"Oh really, whereabouts"?

"Oregon, a prisoner of war. I like it there, want to stay, but they release me and send me back. Someday I go back to Oregon ... maybe."

"Good luck. Er ... any other foreigners here, I mean besides myself?"

"Not like you, not American, fuckin' Polacks.

"Oh, you mean Poles?" I looked at my watch, I was already supposed to be back in the safe house reporting what I found out. I bought the guy a beer, said *Auf wiedersehen* and boarded a bus back to Munich. The second lieutenant wasn't happy. You're an hour late and you didn't salute," he yelled.

"I'm in civies, so I shouldn't salute." *(asshole)* I gave him the camera, told him there were Poles in the second town, and left without saluting or calling him "sir." I found out later that one of the other guys — who spoke German — discovered that the bridge was mined in case the Russians invaded so it could be blown up, and that here was a company of Polish refugees who worked for the Americans somehow in the second town. Kind of brilliant compared to my meager report. I mention this, because it turns out to be important later, because that lieutenant wrote in my file: "doesn't obey orders."

Then I was sent to a place called Camp King in Oberursel, a suburb of Frankfurt, as a trained intelligence analyst, according to the army. This is where I began to learn German. My method was simple. I bought a book, studied the grammar, which is complicated compared to English, but child's play compared to Russian. To study a foreign language in the country where the natives actually speak it is an incomparable advantage. I started by memorizing a simple phrase. (Pronunciation was easy because German is phonetic, as opposed to English and French, for example. Although the accent doesn't go away.)

I stopped a guy on the street and asked him: *Entschuldigen Sie bitte. Können Sie mir bitte sagen, wo der Hauptbahnhof ist?* (Excuse me please. Can you please tell me where the main station is?) His reply was sublimely simple: *Ja Natürlich. Gerade aus.* (Yes of course. Straight ahead.) He pointed, nodded, smiled and continued walking. I of course already knew where the main station was, but I must say that if I wasn't exactly proud, I was certainly satisfied with myself.

Camp King turned out to be an interrogation center for East German defectors, mostly military types. They preferred to turn themselves in to us Americans because they thought we were even dumber than we are, and we might do them a big favor for telling us all they knew about the East German and Soviet armed forces and their intelligence services — most of which we already knew, at least the low-level stuff.

Camp King had been a German facility during the war where they specialized in interrogating American and British aircraft crews who had crashed or parachuted into their arms. It was a great place for practicing the good-cop-bad-cop method. We were much better as good cops, and the Germans were naturals at being bad guys.

I got off the streetcar almost at Camp King's entrance and dragged my duffle bag and myself through an open gate. The guard looked up from whatever he was reading and saluted with his index finger. The security situation didn't impress me. I found the company HQ, where I handed my orders envelope to the company clerk, who glanced at my orders and brought them into the First Sergeant's office.

He looked young to be a First Sergeant, maybe about thirty. He read through my orders, finally looked up at me.

"You're a Russian linguist?" he stated more than asked. "You know what we need here?"

"No."

"German linguists. Do you know why? Because we interrogate German defectors from East Germany."

"No Russians?" I asked, just to say something.

He didn't bother answering. "You play basketball?"

A surprise question if there ever was one. "Yeah, some."

"Where'd you learn to play?"

"Brooklyn, playground, CYO."

"What's that?"

"Catholic Youth Organization."

"Be in the gym tomorrow morning 0900." He waved me out with the back of his hand.

I had no idea what interrogation, Russian or German, had to do with basketball. Could it be some kind of test, a try out? I found out the next morning. I heard the basketball bouncing from the locker room while I was changing. The only player in the gym was the First Sergeant. He threw the ball at me and commanded: "Shoot!" I bounced it a few times and it went in from what's called the three-point range today. The two of us bounced and passed and shot for about fifteen minutes and I realized how out of shape I was.

"You're out of shape, but you can play the game," the Sgt. said in the locker room after we'd showered and dressed. "Here's the deal, Smith," he continued, friendlier than during our first meeting. "You can stay here for the rest of your tour of duty playing sports. I presume you can play baseball as well. Right?" I nodded. "We can keep you officially as a Russian linguist just in case a Russian shows up some day, but don't bet on it, because the CIA would grab him first."

"But what would I do when it's not the baseball or the basketball season?" I asked.

"We have a bunch of administrative stuff you can do; that's not a problem. The problem is that our German linguists are mostly krauts who can't tell the difference between a basketball and a baseball." He must have noticed my knitted eyebrows. "Think it over and let me know tomorrow. The Old Man's a sports nut and he wants to know ASAP. If you don't want to have the easiest assignment in this man's army, we'll transfer you to Frankfurt where there's an outfit that claims to have a Russian section that uses Russian linguists. You'll go there — toot sweet."

I nodded meaning that I'd think it over, but I'd already made my choice — probably because of a mixture of romanticism and patriotism, or maybe karma. Anyway, the next day I told the First Sergeant I'd rather go to Frankfurt in order not to waste my Russian training.

A few days later, with my new orders in my pocket, I took the streetcar back to Frankfurt, but not as far as the Gutleut Kaserne. I was assigned to an outfit named "7982 USAEUR Liaison Group." Just looking at the name, what kind of military outfit was that? Well, "USA" could mean United States Army (which it did) and EUR could mean Europe (which it did). But what does a "Liaison Group" do? With whom does it liaison? Maybe it's a code meaning spying or "wannabe intelligence" (which it did). It also seemed to imply that 7,981 such outfits also existed (which they didn't). Therefore, any self-respecting Soviet so-called intelligence unit would immediately surmise (know) that it was an American so-called intelligence unit. But they wouldn't even have to surmise it; they could merely watch us. We worked in the I.G. Farben building in Frankfurt, which we had taken over from the Germans to contain the army, navy, air force, CIA and whatever other spook outfits may have existed. We wore our uniforms; the officers wore civilian clothes. Why? Probably because they had a clothing allowance and we non-officers didn't.

We — Leroy Little and George Abrahamian and I — worked in a room on the third floor which was called the translation section. Leroy was a fellow linguist from the Language School and George was an Armenian (all Armenian names end in "ian") immigrant to the U.S. who joined the army as a shortcut to citizenship. He also spoke fluent everyday but not very literary Russian. He hated Russians almost as much as he hated Turks, so he was probably not a spy for the Soviet Union. On the other hand, the Commanding Officer, a Captain Olshevski, who probably spoke Polish, might have been a Soviet spy because he seemed to me like a ham actor playing the part of a patriotic American.

In the whole time I was in the translation section we found nothing of any intelligence value. Our room was also called the shithole, for the documents we translated smelled like they did because the Russians soldiers in the East Zone had no toilet paper so used any paper that came to hand and was thrown away after use because they also had no toilets. Our German spies collected the used paper, which automatically became top secret documents. By the time they reached us they were at least dry. They were mostly letters to and from semi-literate mothers and girlfriends from home. After glancing through them, we put them in bags to be burned (we hoped) as classified shit.

I lasted in the 7982 USAEUR Liaison Group for about a year, being passed from the Russian shithole to various other sections, until one day Capt. O called me into his office to advise me that I had committed an unpardonable error, and he was therefore subjecting me to a summary court martial and sentencing me to thirty days confinement to quarters. I was astonished. "That's all, Corporal." Capt. O said. I left the office without saluting or spitting in his eye.

I knew enough about military justice to remember that I could demand a special court martial which involved a trial of sorts during which the accusing officer must supply evidence of the charge, whereas a summary court martial was for minor offenses and the commanding officer was judge and jury. However, despite knowing that I didn't commit anything wrong, it didn't seem worthwhile to demand the higher court because the penalty could be much more severe if the army really wanted to screw me. Furthermore, "confinement to quarters" was meaningless in my case, because we lived in an apartment in a German civilian building. We were supposed to pass as innocent civilians despite wearing uniforms. It made absolutely no sense, but that's the way it was. So, I could come and go as I pleased. So, my choice was to grin and bear it. Cowardly, but probably for the best. You see, I despised Capt. Olshevski and suspected he was a Russian spy. Maybe I said so in the German bar around the corner from our apartment and maybe it was true and East German spies who also hung out there heard me and tipped Capt. O off. That would certainly be reason enough to get rid of me. Sgt. Roland also frequented that bar. He was a controlled alcoholic who spouted whatever secrets happened to be on his mind. Whether the East German spies could understand his southern accented slurs is another question entirely. Sgt. Roland had a photographic memory. If one of our sources (spies) said, for example, that he saw a certain Russian tank with a certain number painted on it, Sgt. Roland knew immediately if that tank could be where the source said it was. If Roland became convinced that the source was lying, he just said, "Get rid of him." How he was gotten rid of I never learned; maybe Sgt. Roland didn't either, and didn't care.

One day when I stepped out of the paternoster elevator and bent to sign the in-log, the security officer, a second lieutenant who sat there every day watching us sign in and out (I sometimes wondered why he didn't die of boredom, or at least go mad), handed me an envelope. It contained orders for me to report to some 2nd Armored Division support group. I can't for the life of me remember its name. It was in a town called Bad Kreuznach, which I had never heard of. When I looked it up, I saw that it was located about a hundred miles to the south-west of Frankfurt. I had been transferred there — effective immediately. I wasn't able to find out why. Capt. O refused to see me, which wasn't surprising because he was responsible for the transfer. I really didn't want to go because it would mean leaving my German girlfriend — later my wife — who lived in Frankfurt. I considered accusing Capt. O of spying for the East Germans or the Russians but realized that doing so without evidence would surely make it worse. I packed my duffelbag and took a train to Bad Kreuznach. It was a local, so it took a few hours to get there.

Bad Kreuznach

Upon arrival, I walked out of the train station intending to find out how to get to my new outfit, or at least to the Second Armored Division. A young German approached me and asked in German if I was Cpl. Frank T. Smith. Actually, he smiled and *told* me I was Cpl. Frank T. Smith, because I was the only uniformed passenger to leave the train.

He grabbed my duffel bag and led me to an army car. "Come," he said, "I, Hans, will take you to the x Group," as he tossed my bag into the trunk. You can imagine my surprise that the x Group, a part of the Second Armored Division, had sent a driver to pick me up, a mere corporal, at the station. It was so strange that I wondered if I was being kidnapped by the Soviets. I asked the driver, Hans, if it was usual that corporals are picked up at the station when they first arrive. He said, "O nein. You must be very important corporal."

It took a while to figure out, but I finally understood the reason. They — the x Group had of course received a copy of my orders, so knew I was coming. How they knew how and when, I never did find out. In my orders my MOS (Military Occupational Specialty) was shown as "intelligence analyst." What must the Commanding Officer (if he even knew) and the First Sergeant (who certainly knew) be thinking? Easy: Why are they transferring an intelligence analyst to this, our until now comfortable unit? Because, I eventually discovered, the First Sergeant was operating a 20% commission loan racket. Let's say a soldier of any rank needed some extra money for whatever reason. He could get it from the First Sergeant who, by the way, was the person who actually paid everyone in the company on payday. So, if you had borrowed $20, you received $4 less on payday. Did the C.O. know about it and receive a cut? Unknown, but possible. They probably thought that I had come to investigate the rumors. I realized this when, after a few months, I needed a loan, so I went to the First Sergeant. Of course, why not? Everyone else does. When I asked him for a twenty buck loan, he looked avuncularly at me and shook his head. "Sorry corporal, but I'm kinda short myself this month."

We rode in a bus every morning to another building outside the 2nd Armored Division Kaserne across from a huge laundry building. It was one story high, half a block long with offices all along the hall. The Commanding Officer was a full colonel, a captain was Executive Officer. A major was in charge of the motor pool, etc. I was assigned to Lt. Colonel Moultrie Hanks, whose large office was on one side of the hall, and across the hall was another office inhabited by a Captain, a Sgt. First Class and now, me. Down the hall was the large personnel office run by a Chief Warrant officer, a Sergeant, a corporal and a couple of PFCs. All this to run a laundry? which we didn't even do. It was run by a bunch of Polish defectors, who not only worked it, but also managed it.

Colonel Hanks was intrigued by my MOS: "intelligence analyst." He didn't ask me what I was doing there, for this was obviously an outfit for fuckups, one of which he must also have been. He put me in charge of the "safe room": a large closet containing classified documents. I saw improvement was needed after reading the documents.

"Sir," I said one morning without fear of disturbing him, "I have a suggestion about how the security of our safe room could be improved."

"What is it, corporal? Improvement is always welcome. What do you suggest?"

"Well Sir, what's classified is the plan to evacuate civilian dependents in case the Russians invade from the east."

"Hm, yes. Not much chance of that happening."

"No, but you never know," I frowned. "I guess that's why it's there."

"Yes, of course. Go on."

"Well, it seems to me, first of all, that *confidential* is a too low classification for something so important."

"Does it now?" he said, thinking he had me there. "If I remember correctly — and I do — it specifies that dependents should have at least a half tank of gas in their cars at all times so they can skedaddle outta here at a moment's notice ... if necessary. Am I right?"

"Yes Sir."

"So, we can't call something *top secret* that's known to every doggone dependent in the 2nd Armored Division as well as our own dependents." He paused and smiled. "Can we Corporal?"

"No Sir, but what about the routes leading to the French ports? I mean it's pretty far and you could get lost. But in an organized convoy with a leading vehicle whose drivers know where they're going, that would have to be at least *secret* I think, just in case the Russkies ..."

"By God, you're right," Colonel Hanks interrupted. "What are the routes anyway, I don't remember off hand."

"That's just it, Colonel," I answered histrionically. "There are none. All the plan says is that they should proceed to the French port. Looks like it's never been properly planned out."

"By God in heaven, we're gonna do the planning that's been neglected for so long, Corporal." He looked at me admiringly. "How long have you been a corporal?"

To make a long story short, I mapped out the route the dependents would take if the Russkies attacked us (which never happened of course) — even drove the route myself in an army vehicle armed with a colt 45 because I was carrying classified-to-be documents (my notebook). Before I knew it, I was a sergeant, although I never got to sew on the stripes, because just then the army decided to decree one of the dumbest measures in military history. The powers that be decided that non-commissioned officers — corporals, sergeants, etc. — as opposed to commissioned ones — lieutenants up to generals — weren't getting the respect they needed to be able to boss underlings around. So they decided that noncoms who had administrative duties (had to think occasionally) and didn't have any combat types to boss around would be called "specialists": Specialist 1,2,3,4,5,6, or 7 (previously a Master Sergeant) according to pay grade. So, I became a "specialist 5" instead of simply "sergeant," at the same pay grade. And to add insult to injury, we had a sickly-looking eagle on our sleeves instead of stripes. Col. Hanks kept calling me sergeant though, bless him.

Another of my contributions to defeating the communists, despite no longer sending inept spies over to east Germany, was something I feel obliged to relate here. The Commanding General of the 2nd Armored Division (of which we were a service unit), decided to play war games. You know, divide your army into Red and Blue armies and may the best army win. Officers took such things seriously (maybe they still do) because it looks good in their progress reports if they commanded something in the winning army. We fuck-ups were left out originally, until Col. Hanks had his brainstorm. He asked me how we could contribute to the game. Col. Hanks's brainstorm consisted of asking me for a brainstorm. Thanks to having read spy adventure novels and having a ripe imagination, I soon came up with an operational plan. According to the war game, a couple of 2nd Armored Division Blue companies were to be dumped in a wooded area in the northern sector of the Sub-Area, as though they were escaped American prisoners of war. The Reds were to hunt and capture them before they could reach Bad

Kreuznach. Those who did reach BK. without being captured would receive a three-day pass and honorable mention in their records.

My plan was that we (me and PFC soon to be corporal Ted Jung — yes, I had an assistant by then, with whom I spent endless duty hours playing chess) would play the part of the local underground. We would assist the escapees by bringing them back to Bad Kreuznach in a vehicle, if they were able to contact us. If they had to walk all the way it would take two days and they only had k-rations and weren't allowed to have money on them.

Ted and I got a map of the area, followed the road north with a pencil to about a quarter of the way from the escapee's drop-off point, measured three kilometers into the woods and marked an X. We copied the coordinates and decided it would take us about a half hour to walk to X from the road where we would leave the van which we would get from the motor pool. We calculated the time it would take the escapees to walk there to be about two hours, by which time we would be there waiting for them. We would then lead them back to the road and the van and then back to Bad Kreuznach. If there were more than we had room for we could always return for them.

Col. Hanks was delighted. He showed the plan to the Commanding General who, although he may not have been delighted, decided he had nothing to lose and approved it. We briefed the escapees the night before their drop-off, telling them if they could get to X (we gave them the coordinates and landmarks from the map) their troubles were over. We would transport them in comfort to freedom army style.

The next morning Ted and I slept in late; we didn't have to be at the rendezvous (X) for a couple of hours according to our calculations. I dressed in my Bogart getup, fedora hat and all, and was quite pleased with myself. Ted looked much more German than I in lederhosen, but we laughed at each other.

It took us two hours to reach the spot where we were to leave the van, almost an hour more than planned. How were we to know it wouldn't go more than 60 kms. per hour? Then what we plunged into was more like a jungle than woods, overgrown with bushes and trees and hard going. We had a compass which we hoped would lead us directly to the spot (X) where we were supposed to wait for the Yanks who had so cleverly escaped from the Krauts. Actually, Krauts weren't the enemy anymore, but it was hard to imagine Russians in a German jungle. We were hampered by hills and dales, rocks, shrubs and detours, but by sheer will and luck we finally reached the meeting point (X) although it took us three hours instead of thirty minutes. Four guys were lounging on a slope.

"Jeez," one said, "it took you guys long enough."

"What happened to the rest," Ted asked. "Captured?"

"Nah, they got tired of waiting and went south. You guys are four hours late."

"Yeah, well, the Krauts came to our village looking for you guys and we had to hide in a cellar till they left," I explained.

"What Krauts? I thought they were supposed to be Russkies," a runt with ears like Dumbo said.

"Whatever."

"Oh, I get it. All part of the war game, right?"

"Right," Ted said. "You guys gotta learn patience. We're glad you four got patience, so we'll give you a special mention."

"Fuck the mention," a wise guy said. "Let's get outta here. I'm freezing my ass off."

Ted and I were drenched in sweat. "Wait a couple of minutes," I said. "We have to rest."

"How far is the vee-hicle?"

78

"About two kilometers."

"But not as the crow flies," Ted added.

"What crow?" Dumbo asked.

We kept up the conversation a few minutes more in order to rest, but finally had to get started, and not only because our escapees were anxious to move. We had no idea how long it would take us to get back to the road and our van, and the day was waning.

"Hey, something's wrong with the compass," Ted said after we'd only gone a few steps.

"What now?" I groaned.

"The needle doesn't move."

"Lemme see that," Dumbo said. "He flicked it hard with his thumb as though he was playing marbles. He shook it a bit and said, "It was stuck, that's all. Which way we goin'?"

"West-Northwest," Ted told him.

"That's all? Nothin' more exact than that?"

"Well no, we came east-south-east, so we gotta go back the opposite."

"Yeah, you could find Paris that way. What are we lookin' for?"

"Never mind," I interrupted, "let's just go or we won't get anywhere." I figured we'd have to at least hit the road, even if not exactly where the van was.

It got dark much quicker than we expected, and our situation looked dark as well. The escapees were equipped to spend the night outdoors, but Ted and I definitely weren't. It was almost pitch black, no moon, when we spotted a light ahead. The others stopped complaining and one of them said, "Are we there?"

We didn't answer him, just stumbled towards the light.

It turned out to be a Gasthaus on the other side of a road. As we crossed it Ted said, "Hey Frank, this is a pretty skimpy road. The one we parked the van on was much wider."

I had noticed that but didn't want to think about it. "Maybe it narrows down farther up north than we got," I said, and hoped.

Inside the Gasthaus it was warm and cozy looking. Five or six Germans were seated around a *Stammtisch* drinking beer and playing cards. They were laughing and smoking and joking around, obviously not paying much attention to the game. We must have looked like men from Mars to them. They shut up and stared at us open-mouthed. A young beauteous Fräulein was behind the bar leaning over with her chin on her hand. She wore a dirndl cut low pushing up her breasts. Ted and I approached her.

"Is this the road to Bad Kreuznach?"

She smiled. "No, it's the road to the road to Bad Kreuznach."

"Oh," I said, puzzled. "And how far is it from the road to the road to Bad Kreuznach to the road to Bad Kreuznach?"

The Germans were all listening of course, and they burst out laughing. "Beer for the Amis!" one of them shouted. The girl moved to the middle of the bar and began pouring steins of tap beer. The grunts didn't speak German, but they understood Bier and Amis, so they rushed to the bar. We were all thirsty. We turned to our benefactors, raised our glasses and said, Prost! They returned the toast with deafening shouts.

"It's about ten kilometers to that main road," the barmaid said.

"Ten kilometers!"

"Yes, it's only about two through the woods, but no one would go through the woods at night."

We downed our beer and I said to Ted, "We should buy them one back. I have ten marks, how about you?" Ted was a thrifty person, I knew, and foreseeing. In other words, he always had money on him.

"No problem," he said.

"Beer for our friends," I told the girl, who looked familiar. "What's your name?"

"Heidi."

"Really?"

"Yes, it's a ridiculous name. I'm going to change it as soon as I get out of here. I'm going to the university soon."

"A rose by any other name would smell as sweet," I tried to say in German, hoping that it didn't get skewed. I guess it didn't for she smiled as sweetly as a rose.

"Which university is that?"

"Mainz," she replied.

"That's not so far."

"Not far enough," she said.

Then it hit me. "Do you know who you look like?"

"Who?"

"Ingrid Bergman."

"Oh? Who's that?"

"I'm starving," one of the grunts said. He had his knapsack full of k-rations and he was starving? No, but I was.

"What do you say we get something to eat," I asked Ted. "I'll pay you back my half on payday. These guys don't have any money."

"Well," Ted said, "we're the underground so I guess we can do whatever we want."

"Damn right. Heidi, do you have anything to eat?"

"We only have *Wiener Schnitzel mit Kartoffelsalat*," she said. "It's very good."

My mouth watered. "Great. Sechs Schnitzels mit Kartoffelsalat."

"Papa," she cried into the kitchen, and repeated the order.

One thing led to another, and we were soon fraternizing with our new friends, our bellies full and half drunk on real German beer, which is not the piss you get in the States with German labels. When Ted asked the Germans if they wanted to join the underground, I knew it was time to go. I had spent much of the time at the bar shooting the breeze with Heidi. I got her phone number and directions to the Gasthaus. She was only eighteen, but what the hell, I wasn't much older. I invited her to see a great movie with the beautiful actress whom she resembled. She wanted to know when and where.

"I'll find out," I said. "Maybe in Mainz." If I didn't have a girlfriend waiting in Frankfurt, I probably would have,

She called a taxi for us; we drove the roundabout ten kilometers to the main road and eventually found the van. We loaded our drunken living cargo into it and somehow made it back to the Kaserne in Bad Kreuznach without incident.

As we drove to the second rendezvous (X2) the next day Ted said, "What if the Reds captured some of those Blue guys yesterday and they squealed under interrogation?"

"Squealed what?"

"Where the second day meeting point is."

"Nah, they only have to give their names, rank and serial numbers. Geneva Convention."

"I guess you're right," Ted said, but he didn't sound convinced.

I wasn't right.

The meeting point was the square of a village not very far from Bad Kreuznach. We had never been there and weren't even sure it had a square. But we figured there was no reason for it to be an exception. All German villages have a central square with a statue of Goethe or Schiller, or if it had had Hitler, an empty pedestal. We parked the van on the side of the road in front of a curve in order to walk the rest of the way into town like two casual German citizens.

"You don't look very German in that getup, Frank," Ted remarked as we strolled towards the curve.

"Play it again, Sam," I rejoined and whistled *As Time Goes By*. It was a beautiful sunny spring day, and I was feeling good for the first time since being transferred to Bad Kreuznach. You should understand that compared to Berlin Bad Kreuznach is God's Little Acre. It had only one mechanical traffic light that was wound up like a clock. Although Americans were still gladly tolerated (there were more 2nd Armored Division troops than German inhabitants), we weren't loved like in Berlin, surrounded as it was by the Soviet army. And for a girl to be seen going out in Bad Kreuznach with an American soldier was not good for her reputation. They figured we had only one thing on our minds ... and they were right.

We strolled into the sharp curve and found ourselves being stared at by a squad of Red soldiers lounging around the Schiller statue. We froze. "Keep walking, act natural," I said. They waited until we tried to casually pass them by, then the sergeant stood up and rudely said, "Where do you guys think you're going?"

"Nix sprechen der English," Ted said, and the whole squad roared with laughter; one even fell down and rolled from side to side holding his belly.

They made us get into the back of a truck and we all proceeded back to headquarters where we were to be interrogated by a lieutenant.

"We gotta pick up the van, lieutenant."

"What van?"

"The van we got from the motor pool, government property. It's still parked outside that town where we were captured."

"Why didn't you bring it back when you were there?"

"Well, first of all, we didn't want it falling into enemy hands. And anyway, that asshole sergeant was laughing so hard he wouldn't have agreed."

The Lt. was shaking his head. "Okay, get the fuck outta here."

We didn't go back to the van that night, of course. PX beer had only made us thirsty for real German beer, so we went to the only bar in town to relax after a successful mission during which not a shot was fired. We returned to the van the next morning in my scooter and Ted drove the van back to Bad Kreuznach. The four guys we rescued got their three-day passes and Ted was promoted to corporal ... I mean spec 4.

To make a long story short, I got married. You see, when I was transferred to Bad Kreuznach I had to leave my German girlfriend in Frankfurt — the main reason I didn't want to leave — so I drove up there almost every weekend in my motor scooter. It had a U.S. Army license plate, which was an advantage those days. Most Germans basically loved us because, after all, we were protecting them from the Russians. Vietnam hadn't happened yet. Now, as my army time was getting short, I had some deciding to do. As you may know, when you're in love you do strange things.

Capt. Clark, the only nice guy officer I ever met, loaned me his tux and Renate and I got married in a Lutheran church in Frankfurt, and then in the city hall. Back in Bad Kreuznach, as a married non-commissioned officer I was entitled to free living quarters. So we moved into a three-room apartment in the 2nd Division housing area.

When my time was up we took the train to Frankfurt to say goodbye to Renate's parents, then another train to Bremerhaven and a boat to New York. It was the same kind of "liberty ship" I'd come across on, but this time instead of suffering the pangs of seasickness in the belly of the whale with the rest of the grunts, we had a cabin with private bath and ate our meals in the officer and noncom dining room. The food and the service were excellent. Our waiter, who was also from Brooklyn and with whom we remained friendly after the trip, was black by the way.

New York

When we docked in New York harbor I got on the line of soldiers waiting to sign out. But I saw my parents waiting on the dock and I couldn't very well send Renate down alone, so I got off the line, took her hand and we strolled down the gangplank. The corporal (sorry "specialist 4") signing out called "hey, where ya goin'?" "Home," I answered, "see ya tomorra," thus picking up my old Brooklyn accent.

I enrolled in Brooklyn College at night, in the day working at a variety of jobs. I took courses in physics, political science and anthropology, the last being the only one I found interesting. Renate got a job right away with Swissair reservations based on her previous experience working for SAS in Germany and her excellent English.

At the streetcar and traffic center a few blocks from Brooklyn College there was an Air Force recruiting station. A Staff Sergeant welcomed me like his long-lost best friend when I walked in claiming curiosity about volunteering for flight school. My idea was to enlist for four years, learn to fly, then get out and get a job as a commercial airline pilot, although I didn't tell him that. He told me

I would keep my army pay-grade, that in that respect it was like re-enlisting, but in this case for flight school. I'd have to take a physical and appear before a board, but all that's just bureaucratic. (I found out not only here but also when applying for civilian employment that the words "intelligence analyst" had a positive effect.) I filled out a form with all my data and he said he'd call me when he had all the exams and interviews scheduled.

A week later he did call me at home. He said that unfortunately the Air Force doesn't accept married men for flight school. I understood that. After all, you'd have to be totally focused on training for six months without a wife complaining of boredom.

However, the sergeant said, I could join the Air Force anyway at the same rank and pay grade as in the army, and apply for pilot training from within, as it were. Wives are not an impediment for applicants who are already airmen. "Thanks sergeant," I said, "but no thanks. It's been nice talking to you." [click] He must have already known all that from the start, and the rest was all an act to get me signed up.

Thinking about it later, I realized that my choice to become a pilot in the U.S. Air Force would have been terrible had it been possible. That was around 1959. The Vietnam war had not yet heated up. It was only after President Kennedy's assassination in 1963 that President Lyndon Johnson sent 200,000 combat troops to Vietnam, having decided to win once and for all. Kennedy had intended to withdraw the small number of trainers already there, because he considered the war unwinnable. By that time, I would probably have been one of the pilots dropping napalm on Vietnam, Cambodia and Laos villages. So, I escaped not because of a conscious choice, but because I was married. Good karma.

I also considered applying to the FBI, but figured they are just glorified cops, and I probably wouldn't have been accepted anyway so I skipped that. And the CIA, where I thought I would be accepted

— intelligence analyst with German and Russian languages under my belt. The only possible negative aspect was that my wife was not an American citizen. But that could have been remedied by her becoming one. But I used it as an excuse for avoiding the CIA, which I didn't despise yet, but certainly didn't like the arrogance I'd seen in them in Germany. Good choice.

I worked as an insurance investigator for the Retail Credit Co. checking whether the poor people who applied for 50 cents a week life insurance actually existed and for automobile insurance to make sure that the applicant doesn't have an undeclared son under 25 who also drives the car. (The premiums were higher if they did). Renate's employment as reservation agent for Swissair was certainly more interesting and came with the added benefit of free or very reduced fare to wherever Swissair flew — which was just about everywhere.

I began to seriously look at airlines as possible employers. Those days the best place to look was the New York Times classified section. I spotted an employment agency ad for airline ticket agents, so I went for it. Again, the foreign languages helped. They sent me to American Airlines at LaGuardia airport in Queens. A Chief Agent interviewed me and hired me on the spot. The only problem was that it involved shift work, so night school at Brooklyn College was out. No problem. Good Choice.

The job was interesting and even fun, but also often challenging — during delays and cancellations due to bad weather for example. I also made a couple of good friends, whom I will describe now because the experience of their friendship was (possibly) meaningful many years later.

John Rogan, Paul (Hoot) Gibson and I had been working together on the AA ticket counter for a while and we often went after work on the night shift for a couple of beers in a local pub; it was relaxing after many hours of tension dealing with passengers who were not always understanding of delays, over-bookings and cancellations, all things that were not our fault but which we were blamed for anyway. We were, after all, the visible faces of the airline.

The check-in and ticketing people were basically responsible for getting the passengers on the airplanes on time and selling and issuing their tickets. But one day that changed. We were transferred from operations to sales, which meant that along with the above, we were now required to be super-polite to our passengers who were, we were told as if we didn't know, paying for everything, including our salaries. So, you know: The customer is always right — even when he isn't. Sounds easy right? That depends on each individual's personality and attitude. For some it is easy, for others, it's not.

Hoot (Paul, that is) quit shortly after. He was an honest country boy who couldn't abide having to smile at and ass-kiss, as he put it, arrogant college students and shoe salesmen.

One night — I remember it clearly, not only because of the phone call but also because Robert F. Kennedy was checking in for a flight to Washington or Boston. It was an outside call, routed to our internal number. John answered. I saw him talking very seriously with someone. I took over the passengers he was neglecting, as well as my own. When he finished, he came directly to me interrupting what I was doing.

"That was Jane Gibson," he said, swallowing hard, "the hooter died, and she wants us to be pall bearers."

She had told John what he died of, some fatal disease, I forget which. He was our age — about 28. I borrowed my father's car and we drove up to the nearest town, following Jane's directions. I don't remember the town's name; it may have been Glen Falls. It was a long time ago. We stayed in a hotel overnight, after drinking too much beer in the bar, and the next morning continued to Hoot's village, about twenty minutes away.

There was a church service, then we carried the casket to the hearse and followed it to the cemetery along with a long line of cars containing the hooter's family and friends. It must have been sad (I barely remember it), Hoot being so young and strong and good. It was a clear cold morning with snow glistening on the nearby mountains. It was where Hoot and Jane belonged, more appropriate for them than New York City. John and I barely spoke during the four-hour drive back. What was there to say? That life sucks?

A year or two later, after I had quit American Airlines in order to work for the International Air Transport Association (IATA) as a Compliance Officer, one day I had to fly to Buffalo on an investigation. I went to American Airlines at LaGuardia airport dressed in a business suit and carrying an attaché case, which would surely raise an amused eyebrow along with an ironic remark by John Rogan, if he happened to be working that morning shift. He wasn't. The rest of my ex-compañeros were duly impressed though. I asked about John and was told that he had transferred to air-freight. Good for him, I thought, no phony smiles needed there. I never saw him again, until the *dream*, that is.

Back at LaGuardia airport I became an acting PSM (Passenger Service Manager). It was one step above ticket agent, not really a manager, more a trouble-shooter. The "manager" part was a pin saying so on the left breast of the uniform. There was a PSM office, where mishandled passengers were soothed and sent on their way, if possible. It was also used as a waiting area for VIPs so they wouldn't have to associate with the hoi polloi. John F. Kennedy, who was often traveling between Washington and Boston, a connection in New York still being necessary those days, never used it, even when he was running for president. He preferred being among the other waiting passengers, smiling, shaking hands and being generally loved. His initials were JFK, but no one called him that yet. To fly from Boston to Washington you had to connect in New York, so we saw Senator Kennedy often — until he became a serious presidential candidate, and the secret service goon-wall closed him in — but not enough as it turned out.

It's hard now to grasp how a politician could be so popular, and became more and more loved as time went on, except of course by the Cuban exile community in Florida, the mafia and the military-industrial complex. When he was assassinated though, it became evident. The U.S. consulate in Buenos Aires had a line a block long for a week of people waiting to sign the condolence book. And there were similar scenes around the world.

One day in November a snowstorm suddenly struck New York City and a large part of the Eastern seaboard. It was my day off, but they phoned me to come in and help with the normal airport chaos when bad weather hit. I sort of liked working in the chaos, especially at double pay. I started at six in the afternoon and by 9 p.m. the airport was shut down for incoming and outgoing flights — which left a lot of wannabe passengers in the airport with no place to go. If they were initiating their journeys in New York, they could go home. The problem was with those who were returning home or connecting to some other destination. We had to re-book them (on already fully booked flights), find space in already full hotels (finally impossible, so they slept in the airport), try to calm the irate ones, who seemed to think that bad weather was the airlines' fault.

The Station Manager asked me to stay another six hours and relieve the Lost and Found agent, who was on the verge of a nervous breakdown. Bad weather also tends to separate passengers from their luggage. To use the Washington, New York, Boston example, the pax who starts in Washington on his/her way to Boston makes it to New York on a delayed flight, sprints to the gate to make the departing flight to Boston and makes it, but his

90

bag does not; it joins the many other bags in the Lost and Found area from that and many other flights which missed their connections. So, the poor schmucks arrive in Boston and wait for their bags until they realize that they're not coming, so they go to the Lost and Found agent, who fills out a form with the bag's description and, most importantly, the tag number. Those days the baggage tags were attached to the handle by a rubber band — I kid you not — and they often came off. The L & F agent gets rid of the passengers, telling them to go home or to their hotel and the bag will be retrieved and delivered to them asap. Which was true, if it was ever found. Then the agent sent messages by telex — if you don't know what a telex is ... was ... I don't have time to explain. There was no internet, no email, so telex was what we considered super-fast communication — to the L&F agents in other airports trying to trace the lost bags. A good L&F agent had to have not only knowledge, but also intuition.

The young woman I relieved, Peggy, had a supernatural radar. We once pondered over a VIP's bag which had somehow disappeared between Chicago and New York. Actually, he was a VIP because he told me I better find his bag "quick" or else, with an Italian accent. "Try Rome," Peggy said. "Rome?" I objected. "We don't even fly there." (American Airlines was still a domestic carrier then.) "Yeah, but let's try anyway; I got a hunch." Knowing that Peggy's hunches were as solid as Swiss francs, I sent a telex to Pan Am L&F in Rome with all the information I had. The next morning, they replied that they had the bag, but didn't understand how it got there, because the tag read "LGA" (LaGuardia). They sent it to Pan Am at Idlewild airport (now JFK) and we had it delivered to the passenger's hotel — the Waldorf Astoria. A few months later he was found dead floating in the East River. Apparently, they didn't want to waste cement.

Anyway, there I was alone in the L&F office with piles of orphaned bags in the baggage area next to the office. I don't remember the exact time I received the call from the AA general manager in Boston. He was nervous. "Senator John Kennedy's bag is lost," he shouted in his Massachusetts twang, later made famous by JFK himself. "Didn't you get our telex?" "Actually, no," I said, "not yet." A pile of unread telexes covered my desk sent from L&F agents around the system tracing lost bags. It always happened during storms. I was shuffling through them, when the one from BOS caught my eye because of the word URGENT! repeated a dozen times. "Oh, here it is," I said. "What?" he screamed, "The bag?" "No, the telex." "Well now that you have the description, find the fucking bag!"

I held the phone away from my ear and looked at it as the blood rose to my eyes. Then I spoke to the mouthpiece without placing the earpiece against my ear: "I'm hanging up now. If and when you are able to talk with civility, calm down and try again." click.

I went out to the orphaned bags area with the telex in hand and soon found the large aluminum suitcase with Kennedy's nametag on it. The phone was ringing again as I dragged it into the office. "This is Ted Jones (don't remember his real name) from Boston? What did you say your name was?" I told him. "Okay, Mr. Smith, I'm really sorry about that outburst. It's just that this is so important." I couldn't see what was so important about one lost bag among so many, except that the owner was a VIP. "You see, Senator Kennedy is going to New Hampshire tomorrow morning, and you are aware of how important New Hampshire is in presidential elections?"

"Yes, I know," I said. "Symbolic."

"That's right — and not only the senator's toothbrush is in that bag, but also his speech, which will be heard by the whole country. So, you can understand how important it is that we get that bag to him asap."

"I can see that, Mr. Jones, and I really like Kennedy, but we're closed."

"Oh my God! It stopped snowing here hours ago."

"Here too," I confirmed, "but the airport closed for landings before it closed for take-offs, so we have no planes left."

"What about 621?" he asked desperately. 621 was our late-night milk-run to Boston.

"Canceled. The early morning flights will be canceled too. Always happens, no airplanes."

"Shit."

Yeah, I thought, this guy probably promised Kennedy he'd move heaven and earth — mostly heaven — to get his bag to him.

"There's always the train though," I said. I knew there was a midnight milk-run from Grand Central up to New England because in the past when there were no flights to Boston and Hartford, we'd sent passengers there. But this wasn't a passenger, only his bag.

"The train? Of course. Can you do that, Mr. Smith, get the bag on that train?"

"Call me Frank. I don't know," I admitted. "First, I gotta find out if the train is running. I'll call you back."

"No, I'll hold."

I hung up. Then I found Grand Central Station's number on our list and called. As expected, everyone at the other end was in a bad mood, but Kennedy's name worked wonders — as it had with me, now that I think of it. Finally, I was talking to the dispatcher and explaining the situation to him.

"If you can get that bag here on time, it'll go," he said. "Bring it to me, O'Neill, in the dispatcher's office."

I looked at my watch. It was 11:15. "How much will it cost?" I asked.

"No time for that. I'll give it to the conductor. Colored guy, loves

93

Kennedy too."

The problem now was how to get the suitcase to Grand Central Station. I couldn't go, I was alone with the phone ringing off the hook and hundreds of lost bags to reunite with their owners. I decided to try the baggage handlers, although without much hope. You see, American Airlines had terrible relations with unionized employees. The president, C.R. Smith, hated unions. And the unions and its members hated him. The workers did their job, but with the absolute minimum of effort and according to the union contract. The union, by the way, was the Teamsters. They tried to recruit us as well, but we (white collar types) wanted no part of it. Luckily, every time our blue-collar colleagues got raises through contract negotiations, we got more without a peep.

They had work shifts on duty even when there was nothing to do, and there were bound to be several guys playing cards now. I had pretty good relations with them because I didn't try to boss them around. They only took orders from their own bosses. I bent down and crawled on the belt through the baggage entrance. The Lead Agent and three others were drinking coffee and playing cards. The airline didn't see fit to give them uniforms, so they looked like a bunch of guys hanging out in a bar.

"Hiya, Smitty," the Lead said. "No bags here; we dumped them all in the area."

"Just wanna hide a while, Cassidy," I said. "The telephone, telexes and people are all driving me nuts."

"Gimme three," one of them said, and threw down three cards. There were only coins in the pot, but coins were worth a lot more then.

"And now I get this call from the manager in Boston ..." I told them about it. When I mentioned Kennedy, the youngest one, trying to sound tough, said, "Who da fuck is dat?"

"John F. Kennedy, you ignorant Polack prick," Cassidy said. "The next president of the United States."

"A course, I know dat," the kid said. "Just sayin', dats all."

"Send it by taxi," Cassidy said.

"Yeah, but with who? I can't go, and I can't just hand it over to some taxi driver." Lead Agent Cassidy, about 40 years old, looked at the three working class young men seated around him. "Anyone interested in going to Grand Central with Senator Kennedy's suitcase? With his fuckin' speech in it, which can help him become the president of the United States of America?"

"I'll go," a skinny kid with big ears said, and jumped up.

"It's voluntary," Cassidy said.

"I said I'll go, boss."

"What's your name?" I asked the kid (actually we were about the same age) after he had picked up the suitcase and we were heading for the terminal exit.

"Johnson," he answered. "Charlie Johnson. We don't get nametags."

There was one taxi at the entrance. The driver's head was under the hood. He backed out and closed the hood. "Goin' to Grand Central Station," I told him.

"Not with me, you ain't." He was a black guy, very big. "I'm gone home, man."

I repeated the Kennedy story again.

"Why didn't ya say so, lord sakes. Gimme dat bag." He put it in the passenger seat alongside him and Charlie Johnson got in the back after I gave him ten bucks — the airline's money of course — for the round-trip taxi fare. I looked at my watch: it was 11:45. I ran back to the L&F office where the phone was ringing. I lifted and hung it up, then dialed the dispatcher at Grand Central and told him the suitcase was on its way but wouldn't make it by midnight, maybe a few minutes later. He told me they'd hold the train, just to make sure that young guy Jack Kennedy gets to be president. He laughed and said thank you ... to me!

I hung up and the phone rang again immediately. It was the Boston asshole of course. I told him to meet the train tomorrow morning and get the bag from the conductor. "And give Senator Kennedy my regards," I said.

"You know him?" he said, astonished.

"Sure." Actually, I did, in a way. Once when I was acting Passenger Service Manager because the real one was sick, I held a flight to Boston so Kennedy could catch it at the last minute. He'd thanked me profusely, which he didn't need to do. A couple of weeks later when I was back on the ticket counter, PSM badge gone, he remembered me and asked if I'd been demoted, and I explained that I'd only been acting PSM that day. He said he hoped I'd get to be a real one soon.

Sometimes I think there must be some kind of evil entity charged with getting rid of the special people who appear on this earthly scene now and then and who are destined to do really good, important things. They get streets and plazas, schools and museums, even airports named after them, but their ability for accomplishment is cut short. You know who I mean. People like Jack Kennedy, his brother Bobby, who I also knew, sort of, from the airport, Martin Luther king, Gandhi — and others I guess who never become famous. (On re-reading this first draft, I want to add another, much more recent one: Alexei Navalny.) Sometimes we just have to ask ourselves why.

One day IBM, together with American Airlines, began recruiting employees to assist in developing computer programs. It would take a few months during which the volunteers would work with

IBM, still receiving AA salaries. When the development was finished and made operational, they could return to AA or stay with IBM. I wasn't interested. A few months later American Airlines installed the world's first automated reservations system, more efficient, less human. Ninety percent of our reservation agents were "downsized" and the rest, management, were distributed around the system, including to LaGuardia airport, thereby making chances for promotion slim. We received a few ex-managers and some people who had been with AA up to twenty years. I saw my ambition to become a real — rather than "acting" — Passenger Service Manager vanish overnight.

Around that time our first daughter, Beatrice, was born, making a career move more urgent. I answered a New York Times employment agency ad for an "international airline investigator." After several years as ticket and check-in agent at LaGuardia Airport I knew something about the operating end of the airline industry, but not much else. The word "international" intrigued me. I thought about getting a job in Germany. The employment agency sent me to the compliance office of IATA — International Air Transport Association — at 500 Fifth Avenue.

The director of the IATA Compliance Office, Rudolf Feick, was a German immigrant who claimed that his officers were like his fingers, forgetting that he had only ten fingers, whereas there were about forty Compliance Officers scattered around the globe, and I was about to become one of them. My airline experience wasn't extensive, but I assumed he was impressed by my having been an intelligence analyst in the U.S. Army in Germany, and that I knew both German and Russian. He obviously had no clue about how inept military intelligence was and certainly still is. After a month's training, which mostly consisted of studying the massive Traffic Conferences Manual, Mr. Feick called me into his office and said "I want to transfer you to Buenos Aires. Talk to your wife, think about it and tell me tomorrow. The other posting open is Calcutta." I was hoping for Germany, but Buenos Aires was at least better than Calcutta.

I better explain here what my new job involved. At that time, and up until the nineteen-seventies, international airlines were exempt from antitrust laws and met regularly to decide what fares to charge. For example, if both a French (Air France) and an American (Pan Am and/or TWA) airlines carried passengers and cargo between the two countries — New York to Paris round trip, say — they were contractually obliged to charge the same fare, or tariff as we called them. The rationale for this was that if airlines were free to compete with tariffs, they would lose money and therefore pay less attention to safety. In fact, there *was* competition. By means of service, food, frequencies, efficiency — but not fares (or tariffs). However, some airlines granted discounts for competitive reasons. Take for example KLM, the Dutch airline. A lot of people fly to Amsterdam, but not nearly as many as fly to Paris, New York or London. So, KLM (a quality airline) finds itself needing an additional competitive advantage if they wish to transport passengers beyond Amsterdam: price. Argentina, for example, has a large Jewish community, most of whom would dearly like to travel to Israel, if they could afford it. There were no direct flights from Buenos Aires to Tel Aviv, but you could get there via Madrid (Iberia), Paris (Air France), Rome (Alitalia), Zurich (Swissair) and Amsterdam (KLM). The fare was the same. Those days Lufthansa, although they flew to Buenos Aires, had difficulty convincing Argentine Jews to fly with them. Memory of the holocaust was still fresh, although the Lufthansa employees and management were of a later generation. But KLM, with an Argentinian Jewish sales manager, decided to concentrate on flying as many members of the Jewish community to Israel as possible. In order to accomplish this, they resorted to "illegal" discounts. On the other hand, Argentine Airlines (not a quality airline) was to a large extent dependent on giving discounts to everyone going everywhere.

My mission, as a "compliance Officer," was to clean up the market. That is, to stop the discounts. In order to do so, I first had to prove that a particular airline had given one. How did I know? Complaints. If the Spanish airline Iberia, for example, knew that Argentine Airlines (or any other competitor) was giving discounts to Madrid, the manager would complain to the Compliance Officer (me) and I would try to obtain evidence of said discounts, usually by buying a "test ticket." I couldn't very well buy the ticket myself because I was well known as the "IATA inspector." So, I employed Argentine nationals as "intermediaries."

My first case was on the flight we took when I was transferred from New York to Buenos Aires. It was on a DC6 that stopped in Miami, Caracas, Rio de Janeiro, Sao Paulo, and Montevideo before arriving in Buenos Aires with its tongue hanging out. Traveling economy class on Varig airlines (a quality airline later a victim of deregulation), the stewardess ("flight attendant" now) gave my three-year-old daughter a teddy bear (forbidden: economy class passengers could not be given free gifts) and my wife and me free alcoholic drinks (forbidden). After finally arriving in Buenos Aires, I filed a violation report against Varig because of the free gin tonics, which cost them a $3,000 fine. I assuaged my conscience a little by not mentioning the free teddy-bear.

(By the way, around 1980 the U.S. CAB prohibited U.S. airlines from participating in IATA fare conferences, claiming they were violating anti-trust laws. Well, they were, but the solution — open skies and fares — has resulted in a war of all (airlines) against all and the disappearance of many of them, mostly American ones: Pan Am, Pan Air, Eastern, TWA, etc. Swissair, possibly the best of all in service, efficiency and security, also went bankrupt and bit the dust. Many European Airlines, although they seem to be still existent, were bought by bigger guys and only the name was retained. Iberia is really British Airways now, KLM is Air France,

Austrian is Lufthansa, and so on.

Buenos Aires

My predecessor in Argentina, Jeff Van Dulken (known as Van), had left me a local assistant, Osvaldo Romberg. "His face is like warmed-over vomit, but he's hard as nails, used to be an Israeli paratrooper," Van assured me. Well, Osvaldo turned out not to have the described face, which was quite normal, nor was he hard as nails; he was more like the pudgy teddy-bear Varig had given us. When he picked us up at the airport we got on the long immigration line, but Osvaldo said to follow him to the immigration official's desk, where he showed his IATA ID and spoke to the official, pointing to us. The official answered with a smile, and we followed Osvaldo back to the end of the line. "What did he say?" I asked. "He says: Get back to da end of da fuckin' line." There's more about Osvaldo, but it would mean digressing, so I'll get to my first real case.

Van Dulken had purchased a test-ticket to Israel with a 20% discount from a travel agent in Buenos Aires. Two things must be explained here. Travel agents earned only 7% commission, so the discount must have been given by the airline. As mentioned above, Argentina had and has one of the world's largest Jewish populations after Israel, so the European airlines fought tooth and nail for the Jewish market, because the only way to Israel was via Europe. Van Dulken, who had been promoted to prosecutor in IATA's private court in New York, had purchased the discounted ticket through a paid intermediary. He had presented the test ticket to KLM's sales manager, requesting his explanation. By the time KLM presented their defense Van Dulken was already back in New York, so I had to take over the post-investigation. KLM claimed that the discount was really a subsidy given by a synagogue wishing to promote Argentine Jewish Youth's travel to Israel. It was backed up by a letter from the synagogue stating that it had indeed granted the subsidy, as well as by the manager of the Argentine branch of the Jewish Agency confirming that defense. Van Dulken sent the written defense to me for the "post-investigation." I hadn't been in Argentina more than two weeks when KLM's defense arrived by snail-mail, the only kind back then.

The intermediary, Bernardo, turned out to be Osvaldo's friend, so I told him to contact Bernardo and have him tell the truth, that he never received a subsidy from anyone. Osvaldo tried, but Bernado's mother told him that her son didn't want to talk to him and neither did she, ever again. It looked like Bernardo was under pressure from the travel agent, the Jewish Agency, the airline, or all three, so I decided to check out the synagogue. (I later found out that Bernardo received a free ride on KLM to Israel and back, although I don't know if he ever came back.)

The synagogue was in a working-class neighborhood and one look at the shabby building convinced me that it was in no condition to subsidize Bernardo or even itself. The rabbi was a thin elderly gentleman in a shiny black suit. He received us, Osvaldo and me, courteously, but with a certain awareness in his eyes. The rabbi was an immigrant himself, so his Spanish was shaky. Osvaldo had accompanied me as an interpreter, although his interpreting skill was dubious (he had told me he'd learned English listening to Dizzy Gillespie). And when I tried to explain to the rabbi the situation through Osvaldo, it was soon obvious that they weren't understanding each other very well.

From his accent, I figured he was from Poland or Russia, so I tried my rusty Russian, but he only shrugged. Then I tried German, to which he answered with a Yiddish accent.

Osvaldo dozed in a corner as the rabbi and I began the small talk. How I'd learned Russian and German in the U.S. army, that I was an American, which helped a lot those days, etc. He had a cousin who'd been wise enough to immigrate to Brooklyn instead of Buenos Aires and asked if I knew him, which caused me to smile. Did he realize how many Jews there were in Brooklyn? I told him, and that many of them were my old friends. It was true. I was from a Catholic minority surrounded by Jewish kids. I had been invited to bar mitzvahs, even knew a little Yiddish — mostly curse words.

After we'd warmed to each other I told him why I was there. He laughed outright. I showed him "his" letter confirming the subsidy. He stopped smiling. This is a forgery, he said angrily. The signature was a scrawl and wasn't his. I asked if he would put that in writing. That was too much. "I don't want trouble," he said in Russian, possibly to emphasize it: *Я не хочу проблем*, which was understandable because Argentina was ruled by a relatively benign military dictatorship and the country was alive with Nazi war criminals who'd found a haven.

Suddenly he snapped his fingers and held up the letter. "This paper was ours, but we no longer use it. When we ran out last year, we had another design made." He opened a drawer and took out a blank page of stationery. "This is what we have been using for the past three years."

"May I have this?" I asked.

"Yes, you may, but please don't use my name."

I promised I wouldn't. In the affidavit I swore at the American consulate I called him "the rabbi."

I went to the IATA trial in New York. KLM's lawyer said that if the subsidy was not granted by the synagogue, it must have come from some other source, because KLM did not give discounts. The judge, a retired airline executive who knew the ropes, fined the airline $25,000, which was a lot of money in those days, and said he regretted that it was the maximum allowed him.

I stayed with IATA for the rest of my airline career. When airline deregulation came into effect and the discounts that were once sins became virtues, my division morphed into "Tariff Integrity," which meant no fines and didn't really work, and finally "Fraud Prevention," which was real and necessary.

After twelve years in Argentina, much longer than usual, I was transferred to Switzerland, then Germany, then back to Switzerland and, finally back to Argentina in 1986 until I retired in 1998 when I was manager for Fraud Prevention — Latin America. Osvaldo eventually emigrated to Israel, where he became a renowned artist And university professor.

But now back to my original posting in Buenos Aires — and this memoir gets interesting.

We (Renate, our three-year-old daughter and I) were stuck in a temporary apartment in downtown Buenos Aires while looking for something more appropriate and affordable. I had no office, so between visits to airlines and getting to know the territory, I often just wandered around the city.

An uncle of Renate's, Uncle Karl, was an anthroposophist and when he learned that we would be living in Argentina, he wrote to Renate that there was a Rudolf Steiner Schule in Buenos Aires, which we could consider for our Beatrice. So, when I came upon a German bookstore one day, I entered and asked in German if they knew where the Rudolf Steiner Schule was. The owner was happy to oblige. He looked up the address and told me "Warnes 1331 Florida." Warnes meant nothing to me, but Florida was one of the main streets of Buenos Aires. Because in New York, and America in general, the house or building number comes before the street name, I thought the address of the Rudolf Steiner Schule was 1331 Florida Street.

As I was one block away from Florida Street, I walked over to it and saw that the numbering was at the 500 block. I had nothing better to do, so I decided to walk down Florida Street until I arrived at 1331 and the Rudolf Steiner Schule. However, when I arrived at

1100, Florida Street ended. I feared I might fall into the great River *Rio de la Plata by* going on much farther. Concluding that the bookstore guy had given me the wrong address, I shrugged and forgot about it.

There were two German language newspapers: one very right wing, in fact close to Nazi; and the Argentinisches Tageblatt, centrist, perhaps Jewish oriented. We looked through the classified sections of both newspapers, looking for a house or a more comfortable apartment for rent, but found nothing of interest. Finally, in desperation, we put an ad in the Tageblatt in German. We received a call the next day offering a small house in a suburb at a reasonable rent. We agreed to meet the owner at the central railroad station, *Retiro*, in order to travel with him to the suburb of *Florida.*

The house he offered was perfect. It was small, but just right for three people. It also had a garden in the back and even a small swimming pool. The train from and to Buenos Aires was hourly and took only twenty minutes. We took it immediately.

Frank and Bibi (Beatrice) in the pool in Florida (around 1963).

It turned out that Florida had many German residents, most of whom had arrived after World War Two. Among them were also German Jews, such as the owner of our house, and Nazis, something we were to learn later the hard way, for none of them admitted to being or having been admirers of Hitler.

Our next-door neighbors were ethnic German Mennonites. The family told us, after we got to know them better, that they were originally members of a German Mennonite colony in Russia, whose lives were made impossible by the Soviets. Many emigrated to Canada. Others, including our neighbors, went to Paraguay, where they began to build a Mennonite colony from scratch in the jungle. That life was too hard for them, so they continued on to Argentina. They were very good people and helped us get acclimated.

They told us that there was a German school a few blocks away. It turned out to be the Rudolf Steiner Schule that Uncle Karl meant. "Warnes 1331 Florida" didn't indicate Number 1331 Florida Street, but Warnes Street Number 1331, Florida. Warnes was a soldier who fought in the Argentine army in the war of independence from Spain in the eighteenth century. That I had not been able to find that school on my own and that we later wound up living near to it without realizing it, did not seem more to me then than a coincidence. After the events that occurred over the following years, however, it seemed more likely that we had been somehow led there.

Bibi's mother tongue was German despite having been born in the United States, so when she went to the kindergarten where German was mostly spoken, she blended right in. After a year or two I was curious about some aspects of the so-called Waldorf method. The first school, founded in Germany in 1919, was meant at first for the children of the workers of the Waldorf-Astoria cigarette factory, the owner-director being an anthroposophist who wished to put some of Rudolf Steiner's ideas about education into practice. I don't remember the question I asked *Tante* Ingeborg, Bibi's kindergarten teacher, but apparently it was over her head. She referred me to Erwin Kovaks. I called him and he invited me to his home, not far from Florida, to discuss my question. I went in my new car, a Citroen CV2, a small toy of a car and a lot of fun: air cooled motor in the back, convertible. It was cheap and the first *new* car I'd ever had.

Erwin Kovaks turned out to be a priest of the Christian Community, a church based on Rudolf Steiner's teachings about Christianity. I was beginning to think there was nothing that guy didn't give teachings about. The church was in a private house, recognizable as a church only by a sign outside on a scrawny lawn. (Years later a young parishioner received an inheritance and donated enough of it to build a small but well-appointed and artistically tasteful "real" church.) After answering my question, whatever it was, Kovaks asked me if I would like to join a new study group which would meet once a week in his house/church. Subject: <u>The Gospel of Luke</u> by Rudolf Steiner, in German of course.

Including Kovaks, there were five of us in the group. I found the text of Steiner's lectures interesting, but I had difficulty understanding it. The German being read by Kovaks was of a strange style, for me that is. But it was a beginning.

My daughter was very happy in the kindergarten, where she also picked up Spanish from the other children. It had been my intention that she go to a nearby English primary school so she wouldn't lose her English. But she was so happy where she was and with the friends she had made, that we finally decided that she should continue in the Rudolf Steiner primary school (a good choice).

One day when she was in the second-grade, thunder struck — so to speak.

When I came home from work, Renate told Bibi to repeat for

me what happened in school that day. Bibi told me in German: we were in music class when Frau X, the eurythmy teacher, opened the door and said to Fräulein Oehring, the class teacher: Time for eurythmy. But Fräulein Oehring said No, we're in music class. Frau X slammed the door. Later Fräulein Kutschmann, the physical education teacher, entered with another teacher, a man, who grabbed Fräulein Oehring by the shoulders and pushed her into the corner and Kutschmann said loudly, *stand up children and come out to eurythmy.* We were afraid but we stood up and went out into the hall where Frau X was waiting. We followed her downstairs to the auditorium where we had eurythmy class.

I was astonished and very worried. I said to Renate, "*Something must have happened, but it can't be that. I mean children often exaggerate about something they don't understand.*"

A short time later the phone rang. It was Hoffman, a German father of a child in that class. He sounded nervous and asked if my daughter had told us what happened in class today. I said yes, but I can hardly believe it. What did your daughter tell you? Hoffman told me exactly what Bibi had told me. We agreed that something must be done. I told him I'd contact other parents. There was no need for that. The phone kept ringing, but it was the Argentinian non-German-speaking parents who were calling, probably because we knew German and therefore had a closer contact with the various actors involved.

That same evening Annemarie Oehring (Fräulein Oehring) knocked on our door. She showed us a telegram she had just received from the school's Board of Directors informing her that she was dismissed, effective immediately. I don't remember exactly what she replied to my asking what happened and why. Basically though, she had previously told the eurythmy teacher that she would not allow her to teach her class any longer. Why, I asked. Because she was aligned with the German nationalists who now ran the school. So, when she came anyway, Oehring told her that they were doing music in the class so the children would not leave with her. Then Kutschmann came, accompanied by a temporary teacher from Germany.

I arranged a meeting at home for the next evening with the parents who had called and Annemarie Oehring. After that meeting, where we decided that we would not accept Miss Oehring's dismissal, I called a member of the Board of Directors I knew and told him that many of our children would not be attending class until we could meet with the Board.

The meeting took place almost immediately. The president of the Board said that Miss Oehring had been fired for insubordination. She refused to comply with the school's program. We replied that she had been physically abused by Kutschmann and that other guy. They said they regretted but understood that people sometimes lose their temper. Finally, after strong words had been exchanged, the president called a short break, during which the Board members left the room. A few minutes later they returned, and the president stood up and declared that the second grade would be taught by another teacher, whom he named, and that any pupils who did not attend would be considered "free," meaning expelled.

We sat there for a few moments, stunned, Then, however, Miguel Lozano stood up and shouted, "My daughter will not attend class tomorrow, but I will be at the provincial Ministry of Education in Buenos Aires in order to report this crime, this violation, personally." The rest of us applauded. The Board called for another break. It turned out to be a longer one this time. When they returned, they said that upon reconsideration Miss Oehring could remain as class teacher until the end of the school year, at which time her employment would cease. What we didn't know was that neither Miss Oehring nor many other teachers had Argentine teaching licenses. So, an investigation by the education ministry could be disastrous for the school. They surrendered temporarily because of that, not because of us.

109

I must jump ahead now a number of years in order to make what follows comprehensible. In late 1974 IATA transferred me to Zurich, Switzerland. The leading German news magazine was, and still is, *Der Spiegel*. It was and is widely read in German-speaking Switzerland. I bought and was reading the July 7, 1975 issue, and was much surprised to read in the index *Der Fall Kutschmann* (The Kutschmann Case). I flipped to the article and read how SS-Untersturmführer Walter Kutschmann, a war criminal responsible for the murder of many Jews in Poland, including twenty university professors, had deserted in late 1944 when it was clear that the war was lost. He went to Franco's Spain, where he was warmly welcomed and soon obtained Spanish citizenship under the name Pedro Ricardo Olmo. He also learned Spanish. He then emigrated to Argentina, where he became the sales manager of the important German company Osram. When Simon Wiesenthal, the famous postwar Nazi hunter, found him and informed the competent German authorities in Berlin, the bureaucratic process began according to which Berlin was to inform the German embassy in Buenos Aires, which in turn should have requested that the Argentine police arrest Kutschmann/Olmo (who also held Argentine citizenship) and arrange for him to be extradited to Germany to face trial there. By the time the German embassy in Buenos Aires took a tiny step forward, contradicting the famous German efficiency, Kutschmann had long since disappeared and was never found, although he was sighted and even photographed occasionally. He died peacefully many years later in Buenos Aires.

The fateful strands all came together in my mind. I had known a person in Buenos Aires by the name of Wolfgang Latrille, the director (CEO) of Osram Argentina. He was also the leader of an anthroposophical German-speaking branch.

Latrille had retired around the same time I moved to Zurich, which is a one-hour drive to Dornach, the center of the General Anthroposophical Society. Latrille now lived there in a comfortable house a short walk to the Goetheanum. I visited Dornach with a certain frequency. I had even visited him there once.

I cannot describe here now how I felt upon finishing the article. I kept the magazine, it lies open in front of me now as I write this. I called Wolfgang Latrille.

"Did you read the *Der Spiegel* article?" I asked him. He knew what I meant, and he was silent for what seemed like a long time but was probably only a few seconds.

"She was his sister," he finally said. He meant Christl Kutschmann, the physical education teacher who interrupted the second-grade class, as related above.

"And according to the article he worked for you under a false name. Is that true?"

"Yes, but many Germans changed their names in Argentina." (pause) "And I didn't know he was a war criminal of course."

I don't remember how I ended the conversation, but it wasn't friendly. I never saw nor spoke to him again. I had not known of Walter Kutschmann's existence until reading that article.

Back to Argentina in 1966.

A continuous stream of meetings ensued. The following were the parents involved — the ones I can remember at least. Elena and Svend Wedeltoft. Despite the family name, they were both born and bred Argentinians. Elena became a class teacher for many years in the school we founded, and in another which she co-founded, until her death in 2023 at ninety years of age. Miguel and Ana Lozano, Margarita and Bruno Widmer (Swiss immigrants), Vladimir and María Belikof (Russian immigrants), Saúl y Lidia Gurfein (born Argentinians), Hoffman (a German immigrant), and a few others.

We finally decided to try to take over the school in the next general meeting of the non-profit civil association, the school's legal owner. This required a political campaign, during which we intended to inform the other families with children in the school about what happened that infamous day in the second grade. And how the teacher, who was the violently abused victim, would be fired at the end of the school year. We also announced that we intended to install a new Board of Directors at the next general meeting.

The opposition did it much more efficiently. They had access to all the other families to whom they warned about a small but evil group wanting to take over the school. They also had the written support of the Bund of Waldorf Schools in Germany. In short, the general meeting, which was usually boring, and few members normally attended, was attended that year by a record number of members. (All parents were automatically members of the association.) We lost the vote by a landslide. Therefore, we decided to take out our children and found a new school using the same educational method: Waldorf, and with the same teacher: Annemarie Oehring.

We found an old house to rent in San Isidro, a suburb farther from Buenos Aires than Florida. It was a one-story house with four adjoining rooms all opening out to the patio, or garden. It was simpatico, but impractical. The kindergarten was far to the rear with its own sandbox.

The owner, a young Anglo-Argentine who had grown up in the house and inherited it, came to visit every month to collect the rent. He was as helpful as possible as long as it didn't cost anything, for he was far from wealthy. There was an avocado tree in the center of the garden. He told us how it hadn't borne fruit in many years, so he was surprised that it now had so much fruit that you had to be careful when you walked under it so you would not be conked on the head by one falling. Annemarie Oehring said it was because of the children, that the tree felt and enjoyed their presence, for it was otherwise all alone.

Actually, Annemarie Oehring had been reluctant to make the move instead of remaining in Florida with her mentor, an interesting personality named Herbert Schulte-Kersmecke, the architect and co-founder of the school there, and continue the battle. But she finally realized that she had no choice and became the new school's first and only teacher who knew anything about Waldorf pedagogy.

We first named the school Escuela Waldorf Argentina, which was not only silly, but also an error. We soon received a letter (in German) from the Bund of Waldorf Schools in Germany stating that we had no right to name our school "Waldorf" and demanding that we change it. I answered that they had no patent on the name in Argentina (which they did in Germany) and so had no right to demand that we change it.

Someone suggested San Miguel, because Steiner had indicated that Miguel was the patron archangel of our times. But it was objected that San Miguel was the name of a nearby town. So, *San Miguel Arcángel* was finally decided upon, despite it sounding Roman Catholic. Ironically however, that was a stroke of good luck during the later military dictatorship; they considered the Catholic Church to be a reliable ally in the fight against communism.

One day Annemarie Oehring — *la Fräulein*, as almost everyone called her — said to me that I would have to teach the children English, that she couldn't be the only teacher all day long. She needed to rest. Also, she didn't know English. Well, but I had no idea how to teach English. "Use your own initiative," she said.

I went to an English bookstore in Buenos Aires and bought two books. One was a story about King Arthur and his Knights of the Round Table (I bought a dozen copies so each child could have one). The other was an English grammar book for children. I read the King Arthur book, and the kids could follow the text in their book ... theoretically. In practice they listened, waiting for me to translate into Spanish. Either way, it went well. The other book was to learn simple grammar, which we should be doing now in the third grade.

113

It explained grammar rules, then provided multiple-choice questions. I thought of it as a kind of game. The kids didn't seem amused though. On day Annemarie (la Fräulein) said to me, "Why are you using that awful grammar book?" I was somewhat taken aback. "Do you have a better one?" I asked her. "Look," she said, "you have that lovely story book." She meant the King Arthur book, which was indeed lovely, illustrations and all. She went on: "Use that. You read a paragraph or a sentence and explain the grammar behind it, nouns, adjectives, etc." I grumbled an agreement of sorts and during the next few days I tried it. It worked like a charm. The children were fascinated that King Arthur and Sir Gawain and the rest were all bounded by grammatical rules they never violated, even when saving damsels.

I don't remember all the children's names, but Beatrice Smith is in front of

Escuela San Miguel Arcángel – año 1957 - Calle Ituzaingó, San Isidro
Docentes de la primaria, arriba:
Erica Krop, Frank Smith, Ana María Loisseau, (alumna), Anamarie Oehring, Elena Wedeltoft

Elena. Above: Primary school, teachers and students; Below: Jardín de infantes — Ana María Loiseau — maestra

At the beginning, I was teaching English to one grade from 8 to 8.45 one day a week before skedaddling downtown (20 minutes by car) to my official day-job. It was only me in the office and a homemade telephone answering machine invented by a local genius before they went viral in the first world. But as the school grew, so did my English teacher duties. Before I knew it — it was, after all, gradual — I was teaching five days a week, not to mention administration and meetings and crises solving.

One morning I was sitting at the secretary's desk, don't remember why, perhaps she was ill, when a young woman entered and asked to speak to the *directora*. Actually, we didn't have a directora, or a director for that matter, or stated more accurately, we had several. I invited her to have a seat across from me, thereby implying that I was the director. She was a slight, attractive woman with deeply infused worried dark eyes. She had come to ask about enrolling a child, which is what I suspected.

"My daughter is in the first grade in the public school two blocks away," she explained. "She doesn't like it at all, in fact she is often ill or pretends to be in order to avoid having to go." I nodded to indicate that I understood and so she would continue. "We pass by here every morning, and we see the children running and laughing and obviously happy to be going to school here." She paused and stifled a sob. "Why? What are you doing here that might be what my daughter needs?"

I don't remember exactly what I said beyond the usual making lessons so interesting that the children want to learn. I hope I mentioned the most important of the many things I'd learned until then. That official education, that is government run schools as well as private ones, think that the earlier you start teaching children, the more they will learn. So, if they can't read by the first grade they're stupid or the teacher is incompetent. According to our methodology, this is completely false. Teaching such an important subject as reading should be taught only when the child has reached the point in development when it is sufficiently developed to easily learn, thus, to really want to learn to read. To force the child to read before that — usually in the first grade — can be psychologically damaging. Furthermore, we teach "artistically." That is, the individual letters are drawn and colored and animated in the first grade. I suggested a meeting with Miss Oehring. That happened and the child (I'll call her Ana) began the first grade in the middle of the school year. I'm not sure who the class teacher was, but I think it was Elena Wedeltoft. Annemarie told her to let Ana be a listener, seated in the rear, don't call on her for anything, just let her awaken on her own.

I followed the same instruction in English class. And one day it happened: I asked a question to the class in general about some story. The usual hands shot up wanting to be chosen to reply. Ana's was one. As casually as I could sound, I said "Ana?" Heads turned. The children had been told by Annemarie Oehring, before Ana's first day, that she was frightened and timid, that the other kids should try to help her, ask her to play during breaks, etc. What was not said, but what was behind the words, was that Ana should not be made fun of, laughed at or bullied.

She answered correctly. I swallowed my relief and merely said, "Right." The other children smiled, as though they all had answered collectively. Ana was integrated for good, and now loved school instead of hating it.

Meanwhile I still had my day-job, from whence I earned a living for myself and family, which, by the way, had grown considerably: a son, Marcos, who also eventually became a pupil in SMA, and, later, Natalia, who squeaked into kindergarten before we left Argentina.

Now we were two Compliance Officers. Adil Goussarov, son of Russian emigres to France, then to Argentina when he was a boy. He had worked for Swissair in Buenos Aires as ticket office manager, then for Argentine Airlines in New York, then for IATA in New York as Mr. Feick's assistant. So, he knew the airline business. I never knew if he asked to return to Argentina or if Feick wanted someone else here, for I certainly was very busy, even without the school. Besides being colleagues, we became personal friends.

I suspect the latter, because several months before Goussa (as he was called) arrived Mr. Feick himself visited, with Mrs. Feick. He was making the rounds of the many places we had officers. I invited them home for tea; Mr. Feick requested that Osvaldo Romberg also be there. So, there were five of us: Mr. and Mrs. Feick, my wife Renate, Osvaldo and I. I don't remember the conversation, but it must have been quite general. Osvaldo didn't say a word, except when Feick asked him directly, and then he didn't readily understand. He had to ask for a repeat, or I had to translate. The next day he told me the meeting was torture for him, that he sat directly across from Mrs. Feick and the way she crossed her legs he had to see everything. "It was disgusting," he added and laughed. I had to laugh as well, because I thought that he had at least survived. When I took the Feicks to the airport the next day, last thing Feick said to me was "Fire Romberg."

Osvaldo was neither surprised nor particularly disappointed. He would miss the salary of course, but he was not at all interested in IATA or the airline industry. He was an artist. He emigrated later to Israel, where he became a successful painter as well as a university instructor. He was no longer necessary as an interpreter for me, but he was an invaluable source of "intermediaries" to buy test tickets with discounts. His friends and relatives were always good actors.

Laimonis

One day, after I had been in Argentina for a year or two, I had occasion to visit Air France's office. In those days most airlines had well-appointed ticket offices in downtown Buenos Aires on streets with much pedestrian thoroughfare. Almost all airlines were owned by their national states, for whom showing the flag was more important than the profit and loss column. Air France's office was at the corner of Florida and Paraguay Streets, a truly ideal location. I needed to speak to the ticket office manager, so I was directed to a windowless office in the basement. The manager was Laimonis Holms, five years older than I, born in Latvia, escaped the Soviet Russians as a child first to Germany (learned German), then to France (learned French), then to the United States (learned English) and finally to Argentina.

The first indication about something unusual about Lai (for short) was that during our conversation he asked me if I had the time. There was no clock on his desk nor any of the walls and I presumed that his watch was being repaired. I mean after all, an airline manager who doesn't even know the time! No way. I soon learned that he owned no watch. Something to do with Krishnamurti's teaching about time. Every time I met him in his office he asked me for the time.

In Argentina I was known as the "Inspector IATA." As such I was forbidden to accept gifts from airlines, with two exceptions: free and reduced fare travel on business or vacation; and lunch. The latter because someone had convinced Feick that lunch together with an airline manager was when (after wine) information could be obtained about certain market conditions, such as "who is doing what." Most airline managers were keen to invite me for lunch for two reasons (although there may have been more): become friendly with me in order to determine if I could be trusted with confidential information, and a free lunch for themselves. It all went on the expense account.

Lai invited me for lunch at a first-class French restaurant in Buenos Aires. I ordered the chef's special, and Lai ordered something else. While eating I mentioned how delicious it was. He said "yes, but I don't eat meat."

I was surprised for he was such a healthy-looking guy. I was still under the false impression that meat is a necessary element of a healthy diet. "Never?" I asked. He smiled: "Never, for many years."

Thus began my life-long practice of vegetarianism. I don't remember what else Lai told me during that lunch, but it was probably careful, something I also learned. When explaining vegetarianism to a questioner, don't act as though you think he or she is an idiotic carnivore. He asked me to pass by his office the next day, when he would loan me a book that explains vegetarianism. The book was *The Case for Vegetarianism* (or a similar title) by the president of the British Vegetarian Society. I swallowed it whole (pun intended). It spoke about the reasons for abstaining from meat were essentially health (meat is toxic) and morality, cruelty to the animals we kill in order to eat them. A third, most important reason was unknown in those days: the fact that each year a single cow will belch about 220 pounds of methane. Methane from cattle is shorter-lived than carbon dioxide but 28 times more potent in warming the atmosphere, the notorious "cow burps and farts" problem. Raising cattle is estimated to be responsible for at least 15 percent of global warming.

I had always been a carnivore, and more so since living in Argentina, a country with more cows than people and a huge meat industry, for local consumption and for export. On most workdays I had lunch in a good restaurant consisting of a steak, french fries, wine, a sweet dessert and coffee. Afterwards only a siesta was possible. I often didn't feel well or had a headache. All that changed when I decided to become a vegetarian literally overnight, and I owe it to Laimonis Holms. Lai, by the way, lived to be 96 years old. He will appear again in this memoir.

The Threefold Society

I was getting more interested in anthroposophy, and not only in respect to education. Annemarie Ohering told me that the first Waldorf school was founded in 1919 in Germany by one of Rudolf Steiner's followers, Emil Molt, who was the owner and director of the Waldorf Astoria cigarette factory. It was meant at first for the children of Molt's employees and was based on Steiner's educational ideas. Also, because Molt wanted to put into practice Steiner's social ideas, namely the "Threefold Society" or social triformation.

She mentioned something about the rights sector, the economic and the spiritual ones. I soon realized that she had neither the time nor the ability to go further into the subject, but she loaned me Steiner's seminal book: *Die Kernpunkte der sozialen Frage* (*Basic Issues of the Social Question*.) Later when I lived in Switzerland, I translated it. It was published in the U.K as *Toward Social Renewal*. The latest edition is titled *Toward A Threefold Society*, published in the United States.

It is not an easy book, but it astonished me to realize that the same individual, Rudolf Steiner, whose work was the foundation of Waldorf pedagogy and who had spoken and written about angels, devils, religion, reincarnation and karma, had also introduced concepts about how society should be organized and renewed in a rational, practical way.

Basically, he said that society consists of three elements: politics (the rights state), economy (production, distribution and consumption of goods) and the cultural or spiritual sections (especially education). The defining characteristic of the political state is equality; the defining characteristic of the economy is fraternity; and the defining characteristic of the spiritual-cultural sector is freedom. The problem is that each of the three sections should be autonomous — or at least semi-autonomous — whereas they are combined and confused. For example, the political state controls education when it should be a factor of a *free* cultural section of society. The economy should not be controlled by the state nor by the "free" market, which doesn't exist. Rather it should be determined together by associations of producers, distributors and consumers.

Having been working for many years in the airline industry I saw how this would function with airlines, travel agents and passengers together deciding fares and travel conditions.

The last paragraph in the book especially interested me:

"One can anticipate the experts who object to the complexity of these suggestions and find it uncomfortable even to think about three systems cooperating with each other, because they wish to know nothing of the real requirements of life and would structure everything according to the comfortable requirements of their thinking. This must become clear to them: either people will accommodate their thinking to the requirements of reality, or they will have learned nothing from the calamity and will cause innumerable new ones to occur in the future."

The calamity referred to is the First World War, and since that time history has certainly shown these words to be prophetic. I am writing this in 2024 and since first reading the book in 1969 I have witnessed many and more terrible calamities, and the future looks bleak indeed.

In 1919, when the book was written, the Soviet Union was still in formation — a political-economic-cultural dictatorship. Then came the Second World War, more terrible by far than the First. But the wars (cold and hot) never ended: Korea, Vietnam, etc. And even now as I write in 2024 the Middle East is about to explode in Israel's face and Russia and Ukraine are fighting to the end. The calamities have been occurring 'innumerably' ever since. The 'social question' has not been resolved, nor have the steps been taken which are necessary to initiate the healing process. We all too often still look to the political state for the solution to all social problems, whether they be of an economic, spiritual (cultural), or political nature.

While still near the beginning of the translation I began to look for a publisher. I knew that Saul Bellow, at the time one of America's leading authors, was a member of the Anthroposophical Society. He was also very influential with the University of Chicago Press. I sent a copy of what I had translated so far and asked if he'd be interested in writing an introduction once it was finished. I was surprised that he even answered, and more so when he asked me to send the finished MS to him and he would decide then. But while I was still working on it — with a typewriter and dictionary — I heard that the Rudolf Steiner Press in London had a new editor who was interested in reorganizing and publishing good translations likely to sell. I sent him what I had done by then, about half the book, and he made a commitment to publish upon completion 3,000 copies in hardcover and 3,000 in paperback and pay me six percent royalties. I also figured that the Rudolf Steiner Press would keep the book in print, which they did. I wrote to Bellow thanking him for his interest and promising a copy of the book when published.

My interest in anthroposophy extended to joining the Anthroposophical Society. The first anthroposophical seeds were planted in Buenos Aires in two different places and in two different cultures with two different languages: Spanish and German.

The German side

In 1920, a young German student, Fred Poeppig, arrived in Buenos Aires with some books by Rudolf Steiner in his suitcase. He had recently discovered Steiner in Germany and was determined to study his work. He announced the formation of a study group in a German language newspaper and put the necessary fervor into the group's formation. He returned to Germany in 1923, but the group seems to have continued to meet until the outbreak of World War

II in Europe in 1939, when it became politically inconvenient to continue with a foreign group, which required registration with the authorities. The group then disbanded.

At the same time, however, there was another group of German anthroposophists who adopted a different attitude: they considered it "un-anthroposophical" and cowardly to suspend their activities because of the government's directives and preferred to ignore them. This was the "Arbeitsgruppe Florida" located on the outskirts of Buenos Aires, in the town of Florida. It was headed by Herbert Schulte-Kersmecke and had about ten members. To put their ideas into practice, they founded a kindergarten and, in 1946, an elementary school in a building designed by Schulte-Kersmecke. All in German, of course: the Rudolf Steiner Schule. Once the war was over more Germans immigrated to Argentina, displaced from Europe and China, among them Jews and Nazis. The latter were very well received by the government of Juan Domingo Perón. They entered carrying Vatican passports with Argentine visas. Perón even had a department of his government dedicated to helping war criminals enter.

The Argentine side

Around 1931 Domingo Pita, a member of the Theosophical Society in Argentina, found some works by Rudolf Steiner translated into French which, especially because of the Christian content of anthroposophy, interested him greatly. He organized a study group in his home in Buenos Aires. He translated some of Steiner's basic works into Spanish from French and Italian versions. The group continued its meetings until 1942 when, due to the war and Pita's health, it ceased its activity. I don't know if during all that time either of the two groups, the German and the Argentinean, knew of the existence of the other.

In 1953, the Argentine group was revived at the initiative of

Enrique and Lydia Lambrechts. Domingo Pita (son), Antonio and Beatriz Artuso and Arturo Habegger were also part of this group, among others. They published a magazine called "Antroposofía."

This group founded a Waldorf School in 1961 with the name Colegio Saint Jean. The school grew successfully until the founding teachers succumbed to parents' pressure to expand by adding a secondary school. This meant that many secondary school teachers had to be brought in who knew nothing about the Waldorf method and obviously nothing about anthroposophy. Finally, supported by a group of parents who were opposed to the Waldorf method and anthroposophy, they took over the school during a general meeting of the civil association in 1975 and the Waldorf teachers resigned. The school became an ordinary private school with no connection to Waldorf education.

There was resentment within the Argentine group towards the German groups in the northern suburbs, especially Florida, because some Germans felt that Argentinians, as Latinos, had less spiritual development because they were still mired in the sensitive soul, instead of having reached the level of the consciousness soul as they, the Germans, had. Although this was not true of all the Germans, I can confirm that the feeling of superiority existed in some of the German-speaking groups.

There were four anthroposophical "branches," three German-speaking and one Spanish-speaking. I attended the Spanish-speaking one (Saint Jean), even though I lived at the other end of town, because its members were warm and open. The German groups were antagonistic towards our new school because of the conflict with the Florida school. The Argentine group on the other hand, was very encouraging and friendly. They even donated a piano of excellent quality for the new school. And there was something else I will never forget.

Before I arrived in Argentina, a German named Volkfried

Schuster lived here. He was an anthroposophist who made his living working in construction and he was in contact with both sides, especially with the Argentine side. He was very much appreciated by the Argentinians, who considered him a friend who helped them with their questions about anthroposophy. It must be remembered that there was very little anthroposophical literature translated into Spanish in those days. Schuster had left the country shortly before I arrived.

When Enrique Lambrechts died, I went to his wake. He was a member and co-founder of the Argentine anthroposophical group and a good friend. Enrique's wife, Lydia, asked me if I would do them a favor the next time I went to Switzerland. It had been Enrique's wish to give his best suit to his best friend, Volkfried Schuster, who lived near the Goetheanum in Dornach. I had never heard of this custom and it pleasantly surprised me.

The next time I traveled to Switzerland I went to a beautiful house of organic structure located about 200 meters from the Goetheanum, on the street that leads up the hill to it. I rang the doorbell with the package containing Enrique's suit under my arm. A young woman opened the door and when I asked for Herr Schuster, she, his niece, asked my name. I told her, but I knew it would mean nothing to her or to Schuster, so I added: "from Argentina." That brought Schuster to the door. He was very surprised when I explained my mission. He did not know that Enrique Lambrechts had died and, when I handed him the suit and explained why, I observed that he was very moved, almost to tears. He ushered me into the living room to meet his sister, a beautiful woman named Maria Jenny (née Schuster) one of the original eurythmists, when Rudolf Steiner was still alive. In time, she would become the last living person who had personally known Rudolf Steiner.

Outside in the garden a peacock unfurled its tail, as if in greeting. I was invited to spend the night there, and afterwards, whenever I went to Dornach, I would stop by to say hello to Maria Jenny (Volkfried Schuster had returned to Germany, but we kept in touch by mail). Maria died in 2009, at the age of 102.

NPI

I wrote an article for the English version of the General Anthroposophical Society's Newsletter entitled "The Forgotten Threefold Society," because I had not seen the subject even mentioned in the German publications I had been receiving. It was not only published, but also translated into German for "Das Goetheanum" weekly bulletin.

In 1970 or 1971 there was an international meeting planned at the Goetheanum in Dornach, Switzerland. However, despite numerous requests to the Vorstand (Executive Committee), the subject of Social Triformation/Threefold Society was not included. So, a parallel, unofficial event was organized in a house close to the Goetheanum. I took a few days' vacation and flew up. There were about a dozen participants the first day in the parallel event and double that the second day. I met some very interesting people there, including Wilfried Heidt, Lex Bos, Gerhart von Beckerath, among others. The stated reason the Society refused to include the Social Triformation (or Threefold Society) was because it is political and the Anthroposophical Society may not engage in politics, was considered simply stupid. Wilfried Heidt offered to organize a meeting in his Cultural Center in Achberg, a town in southern Germany. It was unanimously agreed upon.

It was a time of serious social and political change. A "velvet" revolution — "communism with a human face" — had occurred in Czechoslovakia, which the Soviet tanks had promptly crushed. Many Czechs had fled to Switzerland and Germany. They were invited to the Achberg meeting, and several came, including the Czech ex-economy minister. I also attended and led a group on the subject in English. The meeting was well attended, mostly by Germans, Swiss and Scandinavians. But afterwards, despite trying to spread the idea of a threefold society, nothing concrete happened.

I had made contact with Lex Bos though. He worked with a most unusual Dutch company called NPI — Netherlands Pedagogical Institute. It was and still is an anthroposophically oriented organization development consulting company. It doesn't teach anthroposophy, but the consultants are anthroposophists who help normal companies with their social — and efficient — development. They had been quite successful in Holland and were in a process of international expansion — not of their company, but in the training of consultants who could then go back to their own countries to work with the NPI method.

Lex Bos had already been to Brazil, and I asked him if he would like to visit Argentina on his next trip. He readily agreed. I arranged for some speaking engagements, for example in the German Club, for he spoke fluent German. Spanish was more difficult as an interpreter had to be used. I asked him about NPI, and he invited me to visit their headquarters in Holland the next time I was in Europe. I did so and was greatly impressed. It was in a large private villa in a beautiful garden. The various consultants had private workplaces, not offices but two or three in each of the large rooms. All were very cordial to me, speaking either English or German. Before I left Lex asked me if I would be interested in working for NPI instead of what I was presently doing (IATA), which I found unrewarding and unimportant. NPI would give me the opportunity to do the kind of work which greatly interested me, and which I thought had value for society and was related to anthroposophy.

In 1974 Argentina was a dangerous place, especially for foreign executives. Certain revolutionary groups, such the Ejército Revolucionario del Pueblo (ERP) or Los Montoneros, both of which idolized Che Guevara, fought for a violent socialist revolution against the corrupt Argentine government and its capitalist society. The manager of Swissair, who was not only a colleague but whose daughter attended our school, was kidnapped by the ERP. After a few weeks Swissair paid a ransom of 5,000 Swiss francs to the ERP's numbered account in a bank in Geneva. The victim was released with instructions to leave the country within 48 hours, or else. He complied of course. Airline managers took to moving their offices to Montevideo, Uruguay. I lived in Martinez, a suburb of Buenos Aires and drove to work by different routes in an attempt to avoid becoming the next victim. We were three in our IATA team by then. Adil Goussarov and Julio De Angeles were Argentine citizens and were considered locally hired. I was a foreigner. I presumed that IATA had kidnap insurance but didn't know to what extent it covered locally hired employees.

The offer from NPI had several advantages. First of all, it was work I was greatly interested in and wished to do. It also got me and my family out of Argentina during that dangerous time. The disadvantages were that my salary would be less than a third of my IATA salary, and after one year with NPI in Holland I would be on my own. I'd have to decide whether to return to Argentina or go to the United States. Either way, it would be as an organization development consultant starting out. Not to mention a new language, but since we all spoke German, the NPI people were sure we'd have little difficulty learning Dutch, which is similar. Another uprooting for the kids!?

Renate was of two minds. Starting over in a new country in a new language frightened her somewhat, but getting out of Argentina and to Europe at that time was certainly attractive. I told Lex Bos and the NPI yes, I would quit IATA, and my family and I would move to Holland as soon as possible.

They scheduled an introductory meeting for us new people. There were four or five of us. I remember one from Brazil, another from South Africa. We met Bernard Lievegoed, the founder of NPI and several other initiatives in Holland. I had already read one of his books and was very impressed by it. When he gave us a short welcoming talk, I was then very much impressed by *him*. One thing he expressed I will never forget. "We are the lucky ones" he said. "We have anthroposophy, so we have a moral obligation to help those who do not have it, when we can."

The NPI consultants did not teach anthroposophy, did not even mention it unless asked. They merely wanted the people they were in contact with to consider their lives worthwhile, to have meaning. NPI was criticized by certain anthroposophists for helping capitalists become greater capitalists. But they were, and probably still are, missing the point. They would at least have to attend one of NPIs seminars to avoid missing the point.

Back in Argentina I was writing my resignation notice to IATA. I asked in it if IATA would pay for our transportation to Holland. They were more or less obliged to pay for our transportation to New York, where we started from, but Europe was still an open question. I would also have to give at least two weeks' notice. It was at that last moment, so to speak, when I received a letter from my boss (not Feick who had retired), who was based in Geneva, advising me that I was being transferred to Zurich, Switzerland effective immediately. Surprised? Very. But upon considering it, it wasn't really surprising. We were three in the Buenos Aires office, and I was the only foreigner, so the one most susceptible to kidnapping. I don't know if this was the reason, we never spoke about it. It was also possible that Swissair wanted someone from IATA Compliance in Zurich. Anyway, a choice had to be made immediately. I had been in Argentina for twelve years, much longer than usual for airline managers. There was always the danger of "going native." We had a guy in Peru who opened a restaurant in Lima that he called "The Cockpit." It was quite successful with the aviation community in general. When IATA head office heard of it, he was told to close the restaurant or leave IATA employment. He chose the latter option. I had been offered transfers previously, once to Miami, once (almost) to Rome, but I replied that IATA needed me more in Argentina, and I stayed — a good choice. I wanted to stay because of the school, which surely needed me more than IATA did. And, admittedly, I had "gone native."

But it was different now. The school was quite well founded. In fact one of the last decisions I was involved in was buying a new house for the school. We had a complete primary school together with the kindergarten, but the original house with the avocado tree was no longer habitable. Not only was it too small, a high building was being constructed right alongside with bricks, cement, tools and junk falling into the school yard creating a dangerous situation. Someone found a large beautiful old house for sale on the corner opposite the *plaza de San Isidro*, which was a public park that could be used for outdoor events, such as physical education. The problem was that it cost the equivalent of US$70,000 in Argentine pesos. For possession 10% was needed, then monthly payments to be completed over a period of two years. We were able to raise the $7,000. But at first, I was opposed. I asked: what about the remaining $63,000? Where is that to come from? I was accused (in a friendly manner) of being a gringo who didn't understand Argentina, where one did not worry about such minor details as the future. An older more experienced teacher said, "If we work well the spiritual world will help us." That sort of nailed it. The deal was made, I signed and shortly thereafter I left Argentina. At about the same time, the Argentine currency began its "devaluation" in relation to the U.S. dollar. During the last six months of the two-year contract, the school was paying about $10 a month in pesos.

I flew to Holland and spoke with Lex together with one or two others. I apologized and tried to explain my choice without seeming too cowardly. Yes, I could leap into the unknown for my ideals, but I had to think of my family, a wife and three children. They understood and thought that perhaps I could work occasionally

130

with them from Zurich. In fact, they had a man in Bern, the capital of Switzerland, whom I could contact if I wished.

Adios to Argentina

I couldn't avoid feeling like a kind of traitor when we said goodbye to our Argentinian friends. We, after all, were escaping to a kind of Swiss paradise compared to the hell that Argentina had become. Bibi, our eldest, suffered most. She was a horse lover and had her own horse in a club. This was something only possible for us in a place like Argentina. Only the rich could afford that in Switzerland.

The most practical option would have been for me to go alone to find somewhere to live, but I didn't want to leave them alone in a place where the police were literally afraid to leave their *comisarias.* So, we all left together in a long flight. It was much longer than expected because Montevideo, the first stop, was fogged in. We circled around a while and finally returned to Buenos Aires. When the crew received word that Montevideo was open for landing, we took off again. It was like a sign that I wasn't finished with Argentina and that I would be returning.

In Zurich we lived in a hotel for a while until we found a house in a suburb called "Egg." It has nothing to do with being hard-boiled or scrambled but means "corner" in Swiss-German. The children went to the Rudolf Steiner Schule in Zurich. Even Natalia, the youngest, went to a kind of pre-kindergarten.

Natalia (Gata) with her mother, Renate (date uncertain).

A new addition to our family arrived not long after we had moved to Zurich. An English teacher at the Rudolf Steiner Schule, who had lived some years in Spain, encountered a young boy wandering around the streets of Zurich late at night. His name was Marcel and his mother worked in a local bar at night as an entertainer. They were from Venezuela and spoke only Spanish. Marcel didn't go to school, so the teacher, Gunver, asked at the Steiner Schule if he could go there. They said yes, but only if he lived with a family. She thought of us because she knew we had lived in Argentina and spoke Spanish. So, Marcel came to live with us, we thought temporarily, because the mother could not stay much longer in Switzerland. She left when she had to, but left Marcel behind. He was eight years old.

He stayed with us until I was transferred to Germany, and thereafter until finishing high school. Then he wanted to leave Germany, for various reasons, I think one was that he is black and at that time he must have felt very much alone. It's different now of course, with all the migrants from Africa.

His mother was living in Puerto Rico and had a new family. She was willing to take Marcel back, so I took him there. Eventually he moved to New York City – always his dream – and worked first as a personal trainer, then got into the real estate business and in time founded and runs his own successful company.

Epiphany

I don't know exactly when this happened, either when I still lived in Argentina or after I had moved to Europe. But I remember it distinctly. I sat on a bench outside the "carpentry" building which is alongside the Goetheanum. It was a clear day and the view down to the Dornach village was of great beauty. I said to myself: This (anthroposophy) is what explains life to me, and it reveals my task in life. So yes, from this day on I am dedicated to it, at least to the extent my strength and weakness allows. Or thoughts to that effect.

Now, you may think that this is an exaggeration or perhaps a self-delusion, or even fanaticism. What follows is from a letter I received in 1978 from Mireya Galvez, a young Chilean friend. A person of great intelligence and deep feeling. It is to show that such a feeling of meaning and dedication is possible for many, from many places and walks of life. She was a teacher in a school for handicapped children in Santiago. I had suggested that she go to Spain and live in a small anthroposophical community in the countryside with people and a climate that could be good for her health. She wrote:

Yo veo también detrás de todo esto tu gran preocupación por mí. Y, yo sé, tú quisieras que yo tuviera lo que mejor sea para mi pronta curación y mi liberación de muchos "sufrimientos", sabes por qué lo pongo entre comillas, verdad?

Ahora quizás sea el momento de que te cuente lo básico y fundamental de todo. Sabes que cuando yo encontré la

Antroposofía en mi vida, fue para mí la salvación de mi vida. Yo me encontraba sin nada para dedicar mi vida, vacía, después de haber experimentado bastantes cosas distintas – universidad, tres carreras empezadas y abandonadas, hippy, comunismo, frivolidad mundanal, seudo-arte y bueno allí estaba yo sin tener nada de nada. Y de repente, inconscientemente, sin quererlo, un día me le llaman por teléfono para que lleve a un niño al colegio, porque su madre estaba enferma, y luego de dos negativas mías, insisten y voy y me encuentro con una niña mongólica, que la tenía que llevar al colegio que tenía Claudio. Al segundo día de llevarla me encuentro a la salida con Claudio que salía también en ese momento. Yo te diré que nunca me había impresionado alguien como él. Yo parecía que no pisaba la tierra, mientras Claudio me preguntaba de mí y qué hacía y qué sé yo, fue algo tan impresionante que sé que fue algo único en mi vida y que nunca me va a pasar otra cosa parecida. Yo me di cuenta que Claudio representaba algo que nunca antes había ni siquiera atisbado, eran muchas sensaciones juntas que en ese momento no sabía yo qué significaban, pero que con el paso de los años sí que he comprendido, sabes que todo se iluminaba dentro de mí, y parecía, te digo, estar yo en otro mundo.

Bueno, esto es para que quizás te puedas imaginar la impresión y mi experiencia que ha marcado toda mi vida. Yo no dudé un instante qué era lo que tenía que hacer, y dónde tenía que estar, y bueno tú sabes también mucho de nuestra labor pionera que hemos llevado a través de los años aquí. Yo, te digo, me siento tan atada, pero tan libremente atada a lo que es la Antroposofía aquí, eso es lo más maravilloso de todo, que no me puedo imaginar una vida separada de todo lo que es el trabajo antroposófico aquí, te das cuenta que es como haber tenido un hijo y saber que aún no lo puedes dejar solo, porque ni tú ni él podrían vivir separados....

[*I see behind all this your great concern for me, that you want me to have whatever is best for my prompt healing and my liberation from many "sufferings," you know why I put it in quotation marks, don't you?*

Now maybe it's time for me to tell you the basics and fundamentals of everything. You know that when I found anthroposophy in my life, it was for me the salvation of my life. I found myself with nothing to devote my life to, empty, after having experienced many different things — university, three careers started and abandoned, hippy, communism, worldly frivolity, pseudo-art, and well, there I was with nothing at all. And suddenly, unconsciously, without wanting it, one day they called me on the phone to take a child to school because her mother is sick, and after two refusals from me, they insist and I go and I find myself with a girl who had down syndrome, that I had to take to the school that Claudio [Rauch] had.

On the second day of taking her I met Claudio at the exit, who was also leaving at that time. I will tell you that I had never been impressed by someone like him. It was so impressive that I knew that it was something unique in my life and that nothing like that would ever happen to me again. I realized that Claudio represented something that I had never even glimpsed before, there were many sensations together that at that time I did not know what they meant, but over the years I have understood, you know that everything was illuminated inside me, and it seemed to me to be in another world.

Well, this is so that perhaps you can imagine the impression and my experience that has marked my whole life. I did not doubt for a moment what I had to do, and where I had to be, and well, you also know a lot about our pioneering work that we have done over the years here. I tell you, I feel so tied, but so freely tied to what anthroposophy is here, that is the most wonderful thing of all, that I cannot imagine a life separated

135

from all the anthroposophical work here, you realize that it is
like having had a child and knowing that you still cannot leave
him alone, because neither you nor he could live apart.]

Mireya died of cancer at thirty years of age on Easter Sunday
1979.

Mireya.

The Anthroposophical Society

As I gradually got to know the school in Zurich, its teachers that is, I also gradually learned something about the sad history of the Anthroposophical Society. It's much too complicated to go into in any depth here, so what I write will be a synopsis. Most of the teachers and all of the Board members of the school were not members of the General Anthroposophical Society in Dornach. Rather, they had their own anthroposophical society: "Anthroposophische Vereinigung in der Schweiz" (the Anthroposophical Association in Switzerland). Not only that, they were virulently opposed to the General Anthroposophical Society. I asked why.

Since Rudolf Steiner's death in 1925 there had been an ongoing dispute concerning the ownership of his literary legacy. Marie Steiner, his widow, by the very fact of such widowhood, as well as a will, would seem to be the rightful owner. However, the G.A.S. claimed that the lectures, which constitute most of his literary work, were the property of that Society, because they were given within the confines of said Society and he always meant them to belong to the Society. Marie did not agree and she, together with like-minded friends, continued to transliterate the stenographic lecture notes and publish them in handsome, hardcover editions, mostly financed by donations. And if the General Anthroposophical Society wished to sell them in the Goetheanum bookstore, they would have to purchase them from the rightful owner and publisher: Marie Steiner — with bookseller's discount of course. They refused to do so and finally went to court: The General Anthroposophical Society vs. Marie Steiner. The Swiss court ruled in favor of Frau Steiner. In retrospect, it seems so obvious that they would do so, that one wonders at the capability of the Society's lawyers. When Marie Steiner-von Sivers died in 1948 she had already provided for an organization whose objective was to continue the work of publishing all of Rudolf Steiner's works, both written and verbal, the latter in the form of about 6,700 lectures. The organization is called "Rudolf Steiner Nachlassverwaltung." But the General Anthroposophical Society sued again anyway and lost again, with the same or even dumber lawyers. Losing a case in a Swiss court is an expensive proposition, by the way, so of course these cases were paid for by the members of the Society.

I learned these things in a meeting I had with the then president of the Anthroposophical Association in Switzerland (I forget his name). I wanted to know why they were so opposed to the Society in Dornach. He told me that representatives of the Society, in addition to suing her for the rights to Steiner's estate, had defamed Marie Steiner, calling her senile, egotistical, money-grubbing, etc. There was another reason for my disillusion with the General Anthroposophical Society, which will be described later.

I asked him which group would win, in his opinion. I was surprised when he said: "They will."

"Why?"

"They have the Goetheanum."

The Free Education Fund

One day the Rudolf Steiner School sent out an invitation for parents to attend a talk by a teacher at a Steiner school in Northern Ireland. (The Swiss generally avoid using the term "Waldorf" probably because the Germans use it.) I went to the talk and found the woman convincing. It was the only school in Northern Ireland that accepted both Catholic and Protestant children. And they needed money. The response was positive, but of course it was only the relative handful of people who heard and saw her and who donated. It gave me the idea for a "Free Education Fund." Not free in the monetary sense, but free of political state control. So, the "Fonds für freie Erziehung" was born. Helmut Grenacher, a Swiss, and member of the Rudolf Steiner School's board, was my first volunteer, whom I accepted — a good choice; the second was Tilman Wacker, a German, and class teacher at the school, accepted — a very bad choice.

Besides the Northern Ireland school, I knew of some likely candidates in South America. We sent out a Bulletin every month listing the schools with descriptions of their needs, one being San Miguel Arcángel in Argentina, which certainly needed money. We were able to send them a certain amount of Swiss francs monthly. Another was the school for handicapped children in Santiago, Chile.

But I must tell you something about that school first. Before I moved to Switzerland someone in Buenos Aires, knowing that I occasionally traveled to Santiago, Chile on business, suggested that I contact a certain Claudio Rauch, who was trying to introduce anthroposophy in that country. The next time I went to Santiago, I called Claudio Rauch from my hotel in the center of Santiago, and mentioned who had given me his name and number and thought we might connect somehow. Claudio said he was leading a study group that evening about Rudolf Steiner's *Basic Issues of the Social Question* book and asked if I would like to attend. When I agreed, he asked where I was and that he would pick me up and take me to the meeting.

It turned out to be in his own house. There were four or five people in the study group, and Claudio introduced me as an expert in Steiner's threefold society concept. I insisted that I was not an expert but was familiar with the book they were studying and would gladly contribute if I could. I don't remember any details of the meeting except one that quite surprised me. At the end, I asked Claudio if they meet every Wednesday (it was Wednesday) and he answered: No, every day! I also learned that they had a small school for handicapped children in his garage.

So that was on our list of Waldorf schools in need. Some time

139

later, when I traveled to Argentina on business or vacation, I made a side-trip to Santiago, especially to visit a house Claudio and friends had been able to rent cheaply because the owner was a sympathizer. I was invited to observe a class in real-time, so to speak. It was when I first met Mireya Galvez, the teacher. Her love and care for the few but difficult children was evident and impressive.

The house was on sale so the teachers, including Mónica Waldman, Claudio's long time faithful companion, were fearful that if the house were sold, they would be left out in the cold. Once back in Zurich I campaigned to raise the money to buy the house for the school. The money became available quickly, but not from the usual small donations, which would have taken years, but thanks to the GLS anthroposophical bank in Germany. The school's present and future were assured. It also helped Claudio Rauch have time for many other initiatives, including a school for "normal" children, a pedagogical seminary, courses for medical doctors, and more.

Another initiative we were helping was Ute Craemer's *Favela Monte Azul* in Sao Paulo, Brazil. I was in Sao Paulo one day and met with Pedro Schmidt, a businessman who was also connected with NPI. When I mentioned the Free Education Fund, he said then I must meet Ute Craemer, a teacher in the Sao Paulo Waldorf School who also worked in a favela (slum). I went to the Sao Paulo Waldorf School and found Ute Craemer. I asked her about her work in the favela and she invited me to come to a meeting there that evening.

The "meeting" was in a simple one-story wooden building in the favela. Actually, it was a religious ceremony similar to a Catholic mass. A young man wearing a priest-like gown read from the Bible. Ute was seated near him and when he finished, she rose and indicated a large photo of a young boy on the wall in the middle of which was a kind of altar. She related how the young German boy died in an accident and his father donated the insurance money to Ute's work in the favela Monte Azul. It was with that money they

140

were able to build the wooden building we were in. After that, young girls and boys took trays from behind the altar and distributed a piece of bread and some wine to us. (We were about 25-30 people if I remember correctly.) The wine was so diluted that it had only the taste. We ate and drank and spoke with each other — like at a party.

Afterwards I asked Ute: what was *that*? She explained that there was a shortage of priests in Brazil, so in rural areas the eldest son of a family acted as a surrogate priest. Ute was about to quit her job as a teacher in the Waldorf school and dedicate herself full-time to Monte Azul (which was neither blue nor on a hill, but sort of grayish and in a valley). That was in the 1970s and since then Ute's work in the favelas of Brazil has grown immensely. Anyone interested — many who are reading this, I hope — can read the story of her early life and work in her book *Favela Children*, translated from German to English (by me) and available from all major booksellers.

With Ute Craemer in Sao Paulo around 1979.

The Free Education Fund was doing very well until IATA decided to transfer me from Zurich to Frankfurt, Germany. I thought I could continue to run the Fund from there. However, that was not possible because Tilman Wacker, who took over the Fund business in Zurich, turned out to be an ambitious pathological liar. He was soon offering money to a new German school that didn't need it, as well as a German Waldorf school in South Africa, to which he actually sent about $60,000 which had been collected for Ute Craemer's' initiative in the favelas of Sao Paulo, Brazil. When I discovered this, I advised Ute, who sued Wacker and the Fund. She used a German lawyer friendly to her who, however, needed a Swiss lawyer to handle the charges. I of course provided the information they needed. They wanted to file a criminal charge against Wacker, which neither Ute nor I desired, because he had several children, and we didn't want to see him go to jail. The lawyers insisted though. Finally, the Swiss court wanted a professional audit of the Fund's books, which the complainant would have to pay for. We decided to drop the case. The Fund for Free Education died a somewhat slower but just as final death though, due to Ute's and my published recommendations not to donate through the Fund, which was no longer reliable nor honest.

Spain

One day in around 1976 I received a note from several people in Madrid saying they wanted to found a Waldorf school there and could I help them in some way. I asked if they had experienced Waldorf teachers and if not, it might be better to have a teacher training school first. They wanted to know how to go about it, so I flew down to Madrid to meet them. Actually, Spain was one of the countries I was responsible for in IATA's "tariff integrity" game (see below), so it was easy for me to arrange business trips to Madrid. I flew to Madrid and spoke there with Sandra Svabinkas, a fascinating, beautiful woman, who had a yoga studio. She explained to me, almost apologetically, that she taught a more westernized yoga, which she called "Cosmo-Ritmia." I later realized that she had invented the name to counter possible criticism by pseudo-anthroposophists who would claim that yoga is an outmoded eastern habit superseded by anthroposophical meditation methods. Sandra was Lithuanian by birth, who had fled both the Nazis and the Soviets as a child and would end up in Venezuela, then Peru. She married the director of a Swedish electronics firm, raised a family and encountered anthroposophy. When her husband was transferred to Spain they separated. She opened her "Cosmo-Ritmia" studio in Madrid and soon had a loyal group of young people to whom she also taught anthroposophy.

I met with that group and gave a talk about Waldorf education and the threefold society concept. Afterwards a young lady, who was not one of the original group, approached and said, smiling, *Hola* Frank. She had a familiar face, but I couldn't place her, a frequent but embarrassing situation. I smiled back and admitted that I didn't remember her. She turned out to be Miriam, the older sister of twins who attended the San Miguel Arcángel school in Argentina. I had met her several times when she came by to pick up her sisters. I wasn't really very surprised to see her, because since the military dictatorship took over Argentina many young people had fled to Spain, which had just emerged from its own dictatorship and spoke the same language. I apologized for not recognizing her and asked how she's doing in Madrid. She said she was fine, that she was staying with some other Argentinians. I said that I hoped to see her again soon there in Sandra's studio, because I expected to be returning. I never saw her again, neither in the studio nor anywhere else. It seems she was a member of one of the opponent leftist groups the Argentine dictatorship had vowed to eliminate. Later her group was told by its leader to return to Argentina to carry on the fight there. They obeyed and were met at the airport in Argentina by the military police and "disappeared," a local synonym for murdered. It seems obvious that they were betrayed.

I arranged for a small group of teachers from the Rudolf Steiner Schule of Zurich to accompany me to Madrid and give a three-day course on Waldorf pedagogy. It was a great success for the pupils as well as for the teachers; they invited us to a flamenco musical in a Madrid theater.

Sandra was thinking of announcing her group's existence to the General Anthroposophical Society in Dornach in order to apply for branch status. I advised her against it, warning her that Spain, having been closed to anthroposophy during the Franco dictatorship, would ring a loud bell in Dornach and they would want to take charge, or at least exert great influence. But she thought that they should not remain isolated. So, she sent Jaime to Dornach with a list of names, and he returned with membership cards for all of them.

Eventually they began a teacher's training seminar with Andrés Sevilla. Andrés was a Spanish university professor who had lived for a number of years in Cali, Colombia, where he became friendly with Luis Horacio Gomez, a well-to-do businessman. When Gomez wished to contribute to the economic and spiritual well-being of his people he asked Andrés Sevilla for advice. Andrés recommended Waldorf education which he had read about in a book by Rudolf Steiner. With the help of "Juan" Berlin, a German residing in Mexico who had translated the book and who had the necessary contacts in Germany, a Waldorf teachers' seminar was founded; a couple of years later the first Waldorf school in Colombia opened its doors in Cali.

When Andrés returned to Spain he made contact with Sandra's group. I met him and attended his public lecture about Waldorf education. I realized that he was a gifted speaker who could do much for the seminar and the Spanish Waldorf movement. He was named "director of studies."

Nor for long, however. Apparently, Juan Berlin informed the German and/or Swiss powers-that-be that Andrés' spiritual master was the Indian guru Kirpal Singh. What? No, not Rudolf Steiner! Apparently, an unforgivable sin, for he was summarily dismissed from his Spanish Waldorf seminar post. When I heard about this, I went to see him. My intention was to convince the original group that Andrés must stay, regardless of what the Anthro-purists in Germany and Switzerland say. But Andrés said: No, if they don't want me, then I am fine with that. I'm very busy anyway — or words to that effect. So, Andrés was lost to the Waldorf educational movement in Spain. He was working as an organization development consultant, but independently of NPI; in fact, he'd never heard of it. He invited me to work with him at a weekend seminar for executives. I accepted and enjoyed it immensely but couldn't bring myself to quit IATA and move to Spain. I still had a wife and three children as well as myself to support, so it simply wasn't a viable option.

Germany

In 1978 I was transferred to Frankfurt, Germany. We already had someone in Germany, but he was being downsized, so to speak. The United States Justice department had recently determined that the U.S. airlines could no longer participate in IATA fare decisions because they violated U.S. anti-trust laws. Of course they did, but IATA had been legally exempted from such laws — not only in the U.S. but in all the other countries that had similar laws. The airlines argued that they needed to have a fare (or tariff) structure that enabled them to fly safely, without competing airlines lowering fares to dangerous levels. But the U.S. President (Jimmy Carter) listened to a university professor who argued that this was merely an excuse to maintain high fares and that by forcing the airlines to compete he (the president) would be benefiting passengers, who happened to also be voters.

I had anticipated this and had written an article for *Interavia*, the leading aviation trade magazine (May 1975). In it I argued for decisions about fares and other items such as conditions of travel (leg room in economy class, sale of alcoholic beverages, etc.) be made by representatives of producers, distributors and consumers (airlines, travel agents, passengers), working together. In practice this would mean that IATA — as producers of air travel — would have to invite representatives of travel agents and passengers to their traffic conferences where fares and conditions were decided by the airlines alone. I wrote that if this wasn't done, IATA´s anti-trust immunity would be canceled sooner or later. In that case a fare-war of all against all would ensue. According to my employment conditions with IATA, any public statements or writing concerning the airline industry would have to be approved by the IATA Director General. I submitted it to him with little hope of it being approved. To my surprise, the DG, Knut Hammarskjöld, nephew of Dag Hammarskjöld, approved it with the condition that I not be identified as the author. So, it was published as "The Associative Principle — its Application in the Air Transport Industry" by Francis Tate. This was because if it appeared as my article, it could appear as if IATA itself agreed to the suggestion.

I asked some airline executives I knew (without revealing that I was the author of the article) what they thought of the idea. Negative. The Swissair guy said we — the airlines — have so much difficulty agreeing among ourselves that it would be impossible to agree upon anything with the other two parties also participating. Several years later, Swissair became one of the many victims fatally destroyed in the war of all against all in the fare wars.

But my new boss, Brian Mayne, a "fancy dancer" in the halls of IATA, according to my Australian colleague Terry Ewins, invented the fancy term "tariff integrity," which had the same objective as "compliance" but without the bad-cop weapon of fines. Instead, I met the IATA member airline managers at local levels who had all been instructed by their CEOs to cooperate with IATA's tariff integrity representatives, good-cops who would convince them of the good sense of not giving discounts.

Anyway, we moved to Frankfurt and Marcel went with us. Bibi, the eldest, had already moved to Germany in order to earn her high school "Abitur" and thus be able continue her studies at university level.

We took over the house my predecessor had in Oberursel, a suburb of Frankfurt. It belonged to the municipality of Frankfurt, which was desirous of luring foreign companies to Frankfurt by offering their executives goodies. So, the house came with a hefty discount in rent. When signing the rent contract, I noticed that it was between the city of Frankfurt and "Herr Direktor Frank T. Smith." I explained to the guy from the Frankfurt city office who brought the contract for me to sign that I was not a director, but a mere assistant director. He replied with a Teutonic grin that if I was the highest-ranking executive of IATA in the country, then for them I was a "Direktor." They could not accept anyone of less status. So, I became a director overnight, as it were. I did not inform my boss (the real director) in Geneva.

The kids all went to the Frankfurt Waldorf School. After high school all three of my children: Beatrice (Bibi), Marcos (Marquitos) and Natalia (Gata) went to university in Germany and afterwards stayed there establishing their own careers and families.

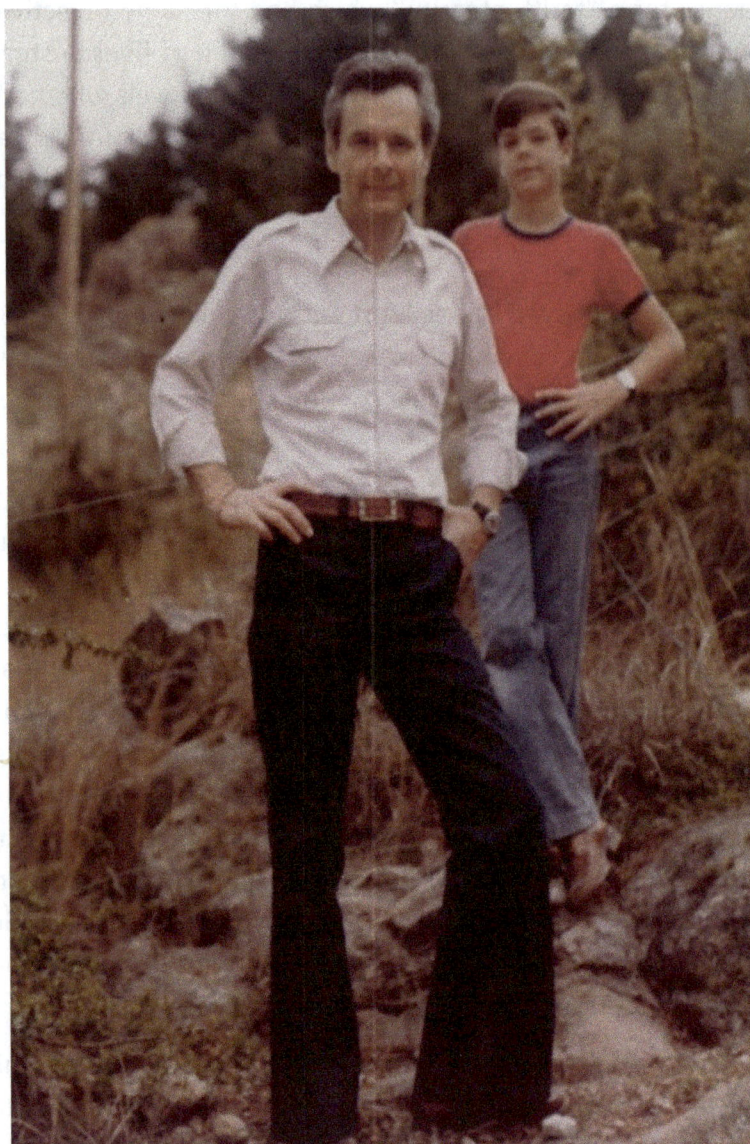

With Marquitos in La Cumbrecita, Córdoba, Argentina (1978).

I ran into my predecessor's problem right away: Lufthansa, the national airline. They didn't think much of tariff integrity, because they had their own tariff control organization, the manager of which advised me on the first day I visited him to stay out of his hair, in other words of course. Well, OK, they did a better job with their organization and power than I ever could. However, and most important, I still had tariff integrity responsibility for Austria, Switzerland, Spain, Italy, Portugal, Greece and Israel. (Arab countries, except for Morocco, were out because I had an Israel stamp in my passport.) More than enough for any mortal to handle. Spain (already described above), Italy and Israel were the most interesting to visit, for me personally ... on business of course, in case anyone asks.

For much of the six years in Germany I lived a kind of double life. I'll start trying to explain that by telling about a play in English I saw in the so-called Café Theater run by a trio of young Americans in Frankfurt. It was in a room in an old warehouse. I only went to it because an American friend had recommended it. As far as I knew, it was the only English-language theater in all of Germany. The play was *The Glass Menagerie*, by Tennessee Williams. I had seen it before, but never with Amanda Wingfield, a faded Southern belle who grew up in Mississippi abandoned by her husband and who is trying to raise her two children under harsh financial conditions, played by a black actress. I thought: wtf? Who are they kidding? Actually, nobody. After about five minutes — maybe ten — you forgot that the actress is black; she is Amanda Wingfield, a very white aging Southern belle. It takes a gifted black actress to accomplish that. And Judith Rosenbauer was that in spades.

The cafe part of the Café Theater was a bar against one wall where the public was invited to meet the actors after the performance. Everyone was most interested in Judith of course, myself included. I stayed after most of the others had left, already thinking of writing a review of the play or an article about Judith Rosenbauer, or a combination of both. I learned that Judith was born and raised in New York City. She met her future husband when both were students at New York University. He was a German exchange student who continued his studies for a doctorate while

Judith became an actress. They moved to Germany eventually, had two children and divorced. She kept the name Rosenbauer though, which made her that much more exotic. Hans-Dieter Rosenbauer became a well-known journalist.

Judith explained her decision to play Amanda Wingfield because, although she had appeared in several plays in the U.S. and a movie, she was fed up with playing maids or African princesses. The Café Theater was hers and she'd play whomever she damned well pleased. I wrote an article for the International Herald Tribune, at that time a marvelous, well informed and well written and influential English language newspaper covering all of Europe. It could be found in the newsstands of most larger cities. The article was about the Café Theater in Frankfurt and its presentation of Glass Menagerie. But what interested the editors most was Judith Rosenbauer (a photo was included) and her courage to play an unpleasant but important character beyond racial limits.

Overnight I had become an important supporter of the theater. All three partners were impressed, but not all in the same way. The article's concentration on Judith made the others jealous and was, in a sense, the last straw among many previous and present conflicts. When I tried to apply NPI's method of cooperative organization development, they all listened attentively to the other, but as a result Judith picked up her chair and threw it at Keith. I realized then that certain organizations needed authoritative leadership: theater and film, for example, where directors are an absolute necessity.

Another contribution was as an actor (stop laughing please). I played the British colonel retired from India's sunny clime in John Osborne's *Look Back in Anger* — until a real English actor showed up — and Willie in Samuel Beckett's *Happy Days* which, frankly, anyone could have played because Willie spends most of the time invisible behind the mound and has no lines.

A more important contribution was my recommendation to present only well-known works by well-known authors, made after examining the financial results heretofore. Who, after all, were the theater's patrons? German high school and college students studying English and foreigners for whom German was a difficult language. This was unwelcome to the other two partners who were idealistically seeking new unknown playwrights and plays. Judith decided that it was correct, and she ruled with a certain disdain for idealism. I also became obsessed with her; but that's another story, which will not be told here. The Café Theater soon became successful and famous — perhaps too much so.

Judith Rosenbauer in the Cafe Theater

Meanwhile, between tripping around my tariff integrity countries, I visited the Frankfurt branch of the Anthroposophical Society, and nearly died of boredom. I was quite fed up with the General society in Dornach, mostly due to what I learned about its history. (I forgot to mention that in 1935 another, even greater conflict than the one between Marie Steiner and the Society about Rudolf Steiner's literary property took place. In 1935 Ita Wegman, one of the original Vorstand (executive council) members, was expelled from the Society along with the entire Dutch Society and a few other countries.)

Then one day I received a letter from Gerhard von Beckerath, whom I'd met at that 1974 meeting in Dornach. Enclosed was a paper by Rudolf Saacke about the previous history of the Anthroposophical Society. I read it and re-read it. Briefly, it described how the Anthroposophical Society founded by Rudolf Steiner at the famous Christmas Conference in 1923 had ceased to exist during a General Meeting of the General Anthroposophical Society in December 1925. If true, I thought, it would explain why the G.A.S. had been so riddled by conflicts and was now barely a shadow of what it was when Steiner still lived, and what he intended. Gerhard von Beckerath invited me to a meeting of a few interested individuals in Wilfreid Heidt's Kulturzentrum in Achberg, southern Germany.

It was the first of many meetings over several years. Aside from Heidt and von Beckerath, we had someone who worked in the Nachlassverwaltung (Steiner's literary estate) in Dornach (Carlo Frigeri) and a lawyer (Hugo Lüders). And of course, Rudolf Saacke, who started the whole thing. He had already been expelled from the General Anthroposophical Society years earlier for talking too much about the subject.

It's much too complicated to explain here. We found by obtaining and meticulously examining all the documentation then available and meeting over several years that Saacke's original conclusion was correct. Since 1925 the members, old and new, of the General Anthroposophical Society believed they belonged to the Anthroposophical Society founded at Christmas 1923, when in reality they were — and still are — members of the General Anthroposophical Society with its common, legally bureaucratic statutes. They had been esoterically hoodwinked. In 1986 we wrote a lengthy "Memorandum" explaining the results of our investigation. The reaction of the powers-that-be was as to be expected: false, arrogant, anti-anthroposophical, etc. The reaction of the general membership was: so what? Good choice. A choice is always (or usually) good if it reveals the truth.

Meanwhile, due to my performances for the Café Theater, in 1983 I was discovered as an actor, and it led to my leaving (or escaping from?) Germany. I played an evil scientist, Dr. Goltz, in what may have been one of the worst movies ever made in Germany: *Das Mikado Projekt*. Well, perhaps it wasn't so bad after all, considering that it was supposed to be a spoof of the James Bond movies. It became a cult flick, staring Eddie Constatine, a well-known actor for cops and robber movies.

A short time after it closed in the theaters, I received a letter from the German Finanzamt (income tax authority) telling me to please visit them with a copy of my last tax return and proof of payment. This was a shock and for a very good reason. I had lived in Germany for six years and never paid income tax. Why not? A good question. At about the same time I received a note from the Das Mikado Projekt production company advising that they had been investigated by the Finanzamt and had to justify *their* non-payment by listing their expenses for producing the film. One of the expenses was payment to actors, which included me. I had received 1,000 German marks (more or less). They mentioned that the Finanzamt might be checking if we (the actors) had paid tax on that income. Obviously, they had not found any record of me, because there was none. The only address the production company had for me was that of the IATA office in Frankfurt city, and that's the one they gave to the Finanzamt and where I received the letter. But I lived alone in a suburb called Bad Vilbel. (Renate and I had since separated for *mea maxima culpa*.) I decided to ignore the letter and see what happens. The predictable happened. A month later a registered letter arrived "asking" me to please appear in their office in Frankfurt within thirty days with my tax documents. They didn't have a gestapo, but the tone was clear: or else.

I went to a tax lawyer of my acquaintance and explained that I hadn't paid the German tax because from the beginning of my residence there I had expected to be fired any day as my predecessor was. He went instead of me because although there was nothing much to do in Germany, I had my other countries (as described above) and knew how to handle them without making waves. As the years went by and I somehow survived, I grew confident and also considered that I would have to pay a large amount in back taxes if I ever came clean. I told the lawyer that in Switzerland foreign management level employees of IATA did not have to pay income tax because Switzerland — especially Geneva — wanted to attract foreign companies. I could say to the Finanzamt that I thought the same was the case in Germany. The lawyer nodded and said I might be able to avoid the fine, but considering how much I earned, he calculated that I would have to pay at least 50,000 marks in back taxes. Which I didn't have. After all, I was still supporting a fairly large family. He said that his calculation took that into consideration. He tapped his long fingernails on his desk and finally said: Couldn't you leave Germany?

His advice was wise and, I thought, unselfish. If I left, he would lose me as a potential client. I knew him, by the way, from the Café Theater, where he was a loyal audience member and one of Judith's many admirers. The die was cast.

When I returned to my office I called my current boss, Daryl Stark. He had been some kind of policeman in the U.S., which the IATA airlines thought we needed to get tough. Then the U.S. government decided that the U.S. airlines could no longer be tough by setting fares monopoly-like and then policing them. What to do with Daryl? The Compliance Director had just retired, so someone decided to send Daryl Stark to Geneva as Compliance Director. A disadvantage (or maybe an advantage) was that he knew next to nothing about the airline business. "Hi Daryl," I said. I got a problem."

"Let's have it Frank. You know me, I love problems as long as they're other people's."

"It's a tax problem."

"Uh-oh. American or German?"

"German."

I had religiously paid my U.S. income tax, despite not having lived in the United States since 1962. Did you know that the United States and Eritrea (wherever that is) are the only countries whose citizens must pay income tax whether they reside in the country or not. Just to give you an idea of who the United States has as a tax policy twin:

> "Eritrea is one of the least developed countries. It is a unitary one-party presidential republic in which national legislative and presidential elections have never been held. According to Human Rights Watch, the Eritrean government's human rights record is among the worst in the world. The Eritrean government has dismissed these allegations as politically motivated. Freedom of the press in Eritrea is extremely limited; the Press Freedom Index consistently ranks it as one of the least free countries. As of 2022 Reporters Without Borders considers the country to be among those with the least press freedom in the world, as all media publications and access are heavily controlled by the government." [Wikipedia]

I explained how these German foreigners forgot who won the war and are threatening to take a big bite out of my personal, hard-earned income. And that a very good lawyer told me that the only solution was for me to leave Germany.

(Not in those exact words, but the essential situation.) Daryl ruminated a while, then said he'd get back to me.

"One more thing, Daryl," I said.

"More uh-oh?"

"No, on the contrary just a suggestion. The ideal place for me is Spain. I know the airlines there and the situation, good relations with the national carrier ..."

"I'll get back to you."

He got back to me the same day and told me sorry, but Jacques (his boss) said no to Spain, that we used to have a Swiss guy there, but he filed so many cases against Iberia, the national carrier, that the president of Iberia called our Director General, Knut Hammarskjöld, and told him that if Iberia kept getting fined for giving discounts, which everyone else does but without getting caught, they would leave IATA. So we pulled the Swiss guy out and the order was: *no more compliance officers in Spain*. I thought of appealing directly to the D.G. but thought better of it. He probably didn't know about my tax evasion problem in Germany, and who knows what his reaction would be if he knew.

Daryl got back to me. "How about Paris?" he asked, sounding happy that he'd found a solution. But I had my doubts. I didn't speak French and wasn't sure if I'd get along with Philippe if he's the top dog — which he certainly would be in his own camp.

"Isn't Philippe Pierquet there?" I said. Philippe, a Parisian, had been based there forever.

"I asked him if he could use you there, and he said sure, he could always use a helping hand." What else could he say?

I called Philippe. He'd been expecting my call. We arranged to meet the next day in his office.

"What time will you be arriving?"

156

"I'm thinking of going tonight. Can you recommend a hotel?" I was hoping he wouldn't invite me home, and he didn't.

"Are you charging IATA?"

"No."

He gave me the name and address of a more modest hotel and offered to make a reservation with an IATA discount. He confirmed it a half-hour later and asked that I not go to his office before ten.

I took a taxi from the airport and checked in at the modest hotel (forget its name) far from downtown Paris. I noticed that the concierge's family name was the same as Philippe's. I didn't ask if they were related because I feared they were. The next morning after a leisurely breakfast in a downtown cafe I entered Philippe's building. Above the receptionist's desk was an index of the many firm's resident in the building. I didn't see IATA, so I asked the receptionist who shrugged her shoulders in a never-heard-of-it manner, so I gave her Philippe's name.

"Ah, Monsieur Pierquet," she smiled and told me the floor and office number. Philippe was a tall, movie-star handsome Frenchman. When speaking English his accent was nothing less than charming. The door to his office was open so I walked in. He welcomed me effusively, although he couldn't have been glad to see me.

Finally, "What's this all about, Frank?" Translation: What the hell are you doing here?

"Didn't Daryl tell you?"

"No. He was positively secretive. Do you work for the C.I.A. on the side?" He grinned but meant it. I sighed and confessed all.

He was relieved. "Wouldn't Spain be more logical? Or someplace in South America where no one pays taxes anyway?"

At lunch we discussed how I could convince Daryl and Jacques that Paris wouldn't work; something about how Philippe had laboriously built-up confidence in the airline managers, especially Air France — so they didn't hesitate to give him information, secure that he would not reveal his sources. And if a non-French speaking American were to suddenly appear it could destroy that relationship.

"And one thing must be clear between us, Frank," he said after the second glass of wine. I just listened. "If you do come here, you cannot be earning more than I."

I tried to decode this. I was reasonably certain that we earned approximately the same, equivalent to United Nations salaries thanks to the D.G.

"I mean officially, that is," he added.

"Aha!° He meant the amount he declared to the French income tax department, which was likely much less than he really earned. I would upset the apple cart if I declared more than he did. I objected that after sweating these last few months worrying about taxation problems in Germany, I resolved that wherever I went I would pay whatever the correct amount was. "And that includes France!"

If he was angry, he didn't show it. We finished the bottle of wine and agreed that I would call Daryl and explain why Paris wasn't a good choice and Philippe would call Jacques, who was French and knew all the tricks, and although he might guess the real reason, wouldn't really care.

I flew back to Frankfurt the same night. The next morning I got in early (9.15), but waited to give Philippe, who apparently isn't decent until ten o'clock, time to call Jacques,

At 10:30 Daryl called. "I just talked to Jacques. Forget Paris." He

158

politely waited for me to object, but I didn't. Then: "It's Geneva, Frank, no buts. Get your ass down here asap. Have a nice day."

Geneva ain't Madrid, but I was just handed a get-out-of-jail-free card, so what's to object about.

I threw everything I had worth taking that there was room for in my little red Mitsubishi and got my ass out of Germany asap. My son Marcos, who had recently gotten his driver's license, did most of the driving. We stopped at the airport, where I went to the Swissair information desk and asked if the lady attending could recommend a reasonably priced hotel. All hotels in Geneva are clean and well attended, but never cheap. I gave her my IATA business card to show my status as a colleague. (The card did wonders in airline circles in those days.)

The next day I reported to Daryl like a good soldier and asked for a few days to look for a place to live. Marcos went back to Frankfurt a day later by train as I searched for an affordable place to live, something not at all easy in Geneva. I found a temporary cabin in a ski village, about a half hour drive to the IATA office near the airport, and moved in. Then I opened a checking account in Geneva and had a check book within days. I wrote to the Frankfurt Finanzamt in broken German with my new Swiss address asking why they were demanding that I appear in their office with taxation records according to the letter forwarded to me from Germany. I submitted that the only income I received from a German source was for a play I acted in for which I received a thousand marks. (true). They replied immediately quoting a Swiss-German agreement about tax on earnings, blah blah and that I therefore owed them about (I forget the exact amount) 150 marks. I wrote a check for that amount and sent it along with their letter tout de suite. I never heard from them again (whew).

At IATA Daryl surprised me by having a desk and chair installed in his large office. There was no other office available in our section, he explained. I wondered if a German jail wouldn't have been more comfortable. The IATA office floors were divided into sections such as Travel Agency Approval, Airport Security, Economics, etc. Our section ended with Slats Slattery's office. The one next to it was empty but wasn't in our section, Slats told me. He had been stationed in London when I first met him; why he was now in Geneva I didn't know and didn't ask.

During that week I had found a most welcome friend — Jacques' secretary, Jeanne, who was located way down the other end of the hall. We both liked opera and went together often while I was still in Geneva. But first I needed to solve the problem of an office. I asked her for advice. She said I should speak to Henri a Swiss local employee who was in charge of logistics; and I should say she sent me to him. I found him in his office in the basement. He was a Swiss giant with a squeaky voice obviously in love with Jeanne. He told me that the limits to office space were flexible. He took out a large chart, a kind of map of the building's guts. He wrote my name in the box representing the office in question and voila! Problem solved.

The Dream

I had an amazing dream during that time in Geneva. It had a strong impact on me. I wrote it down in a dream-notebook (a real one, not a computer):

"15 May 1985

This dream took place about two weeks ago. Strange that I didn't think to write it down before. It was the dream of dreams. It doesn't get dimmer.

I was with John Rogan in a park. We were walking away from a lake when a voice called us. 'You there of the same race.' We turned and saw a man with a light-colored beard and a

160

*woman walking **on** the lake. They were smiling and walking toward us. We started to tingle all over and felt weak with joy. John went down on one knee. I just stood there. A wonderful feeling of recognition coursed through me — and thoughtfulness. Yes, this is it, oh my God. But they stopped before reaching us. It was too much perhaps. The woman said, I think to John, 'You would like us to continue, I know, but ... I woke up. It was Christ. The woman, I don't know. Maybe they were both Christ, different aspects of him. They were dressed by the way in normal, casual, modern clothes."*

I have thought a lot about this dream — and still do, mostly if it was a mere dream or more real. A mystery. Another mystery to me is the woman. Who is she? And why is John Rogan also there? You will remember that I traveled with him to be pall bearers at Paul Gibson's funeral. I had left American Airlines in 1961 and hadn't seen or heard from him since — until that dream, 24 years later.

I never assimilated culturally in Geneva. I didn't speak French and language is the most important aspect understanding and acting in a place. In two years' time I certainly could have learned French beyond the basics needed to shop and order in restaurants. (I could read newspapers reasonably well because of its relation to Spanish.) Actually, I wasn't really in Geneva that much. In order to avoid the nine-to-five office routine, I traveled to my favorite countries, Spain and Italy, as well as several others in my IATA domain, such as Austria, Greece, Israel, etc. I went to Germany on business seldom, but often went there for personal reasons on weekends.

An Important Choice

Then it happened, the opportunity for a choice. IATA's building in Geneva contained several large meeting rooms, where meetings were almost continuously being held. Mostly they were arranged according to airline routes: North Atlantic (Europe - North America), South Pacific (Europe - Asia), South Atlantic (Europe - South America), and many others. That week a meeting of the South Atlantic carriers was scheduled. I was assigned as IATA's representative or "secretary." I sat next to the president — Swissair — in order to answer any questions or comments involving IATA or the meeting's organization. A real secretary was also present to make detailed notes of the meetings proceedings. European airlines present were Swissair, Lufthansa, Austrian, Iberia, TAP, British airlines, Alitalia, etc. South American airlines: Avianca (Colombia), Viasa (Venezuela), Varig (Brazil), Argentine Airlines, etc.

The main item of discussion was fares, called tariffs. All the airline representatives had to agree on the tariffs between the various cities, whether one-way or round trip and many other variations. Some (or many) violated the rules by granting discounts in order to "steal" passengers. Hence a compliance department, of which I was a member. However, since the U.S. dynamited the system by calling it a monopoly, compliance became inoperative.

However, after Daryl left, resigned or pushed to resign I don't know, a Brit named Brian Mayne took over the Compliance Director's job. He may not have been a genius, but he had a brainstorm that was genial. He changed the name of our section to "Tariff Integrity."

It produced mixed or, rather, unclear results. What we, the ex-compliance officers, were given to do was convince local airline managers not to give discounts. If they gave them anyway, we would report such shenanigans to IATA's HQ in Geneva, who would report it to that airline's head office — without evidence, unless we were able to buy test tickets. Of course, if an airline is giving discounts locally the head office must know about it, sooner or later, and if the former, countenance it.

Here it comes: at the meeting in question the Lufthansa guy said that discounting is rife in South America where IATA is no longer present. The president, Swissair, looked at me: What about it, Frank? As I turned over in my mind how to reply I had a feeling that I was in a *choice* situation but was unclear about what the choice consisted of. "Well," I said, "when I was transferred out of Argentina twelve years ago it was before the military dictatorship and the foreign airline managers were being kidnapped right and left (exaggeration) and the Swissair manager had just been kidnapped and Swissair had to pay five thousand Swiss francs ransom to free him and get him out of the country. (true) Maybe that's why I was transferred out, I don't know, never asked." Sometimes these meetings were boring, but not this one, now. I noticed how they were all hanging on my words. "Of course that's all changed, the dictatorship came and went, and Argentina now has a democratic government with a lot of economic problems, which naturally affects our airlines."

Silence, some were looking out the window, others at the papers on their desks. Finally, Swissair, the chairman, said, "It seems to me that we would all welcome IATA's compliance (using the old name) presence in South America once more. "Agreed," Lufthansa said, using his best Teutonic intonation. Others were nodding. "Anyone against?"

Nobody.

"Frank," he said looking at me with a serious frown, "please tell Jacques that we all request that IATA comp ... What is it called now?" I enlightened him. "... tariff integrity be once again present in South America."

My choice, chance was full blown: "Helmut," I said, and motioned to the secretary not to include what I was to say in the minutes. She laid down her pen, relieved to have a break. "If I tell Jacques that, nothing will happen. *But* (emphasized) if you write a

163

memo to the Director General in the name of the South Atlantic airlines requesting that an IATA tariff integrity representative be posted to South America, it has a very good chance of being accepted. While Swissair was nodding, the Argentine Airlines guy said, "And you could add that we recommend that Frank go, because of his ample experience in the South American market." Adrian was an Anglo-Argentinian whom I had known when I was in Argentina. He had a middle management job in Argentine Airlines then, was now manager for the U.K. We weren't exactly friends but were friendly. He represented his airline at IATA meetings because he spoke English and was close. I could have kissed him.

"Good." Swissair said. "Write me a draft memo, Frank."

A few days later Brian Mayne called me into his office.

"Good morning, Brian. What's up?"

He looked at me with pretended scorn. "Jacques just called ... said I should transfer you to somewhere in South America."

"You don't say."

"I asked him why and he said DG's orders and hung up."

"Not very polite."

"So, I hope that you can tell me *what then fuck is going on*, given that no one else seems to know."

"It's quite simple really. During the South Atlantic meeting a few days ago, Lufthansa claimed that South America is a discounting war zone, or words to that effect, so the Chairman, Swissair, asked me why we don't have someone there. I said I don't know."

"Uh huh, and you volunteered to be the knight to ride down there to the combat zone for the benefit of the international air transport industry. Right?"

"Actually no. Argentine Airlines suggested me because of my extensive experience down there."

Brian couldn't hold it in any longer and laughed so loudly that his secretary popped her head in from curiosity. He told her to shut the door.

"Well now old chap, where in South America, if I may ask? Seems to me that the possibilities are Caracas, Rio or Buenos Aires."

"Buenos Aires is closer to Chile, Bolivia and Peru in the west and Brazil in the north. I'm thinking of hiring someone local for Venezuela, if the budget can stand it."

"Very well, Buenos Aires it is," as though he were deciding based on my recommendation, although he knew all along that it would be Buenos Aires. "OK, Frank, when are you leaving?"

I explained that I had to go to Germany for a couple of days.

"Oh, right, your family is there. Going to B.A. alone?"

"Yes, and then back to close up my life here. Today is Friday, by next Friday I plan to be on my way."

While in Frankfurt I stopped by the Argentine Airlines office. The manager was an old friend from Buenos Aires named Siedloczech known as Siedlo, and the sales manager was Hofmann. During my first incarnation in B.A. Hofmann was sales manager for Lufthansa and Siedlo was one of his sales reps. (Times change, as do people.) Anyone who knew anything about the airline business would wonder what A.A. was doing in Frankfurt with one flight a week to Buenos Aires with the routing Frankfurt-Paris-Madrid-Buenos Aires, whereas Lufthansa flew nonstop. Of course they gave discounts to their few passengers, mostly Argentinians. Potential German passengers didn't even know of their existence. I left them alone because Lufthansa couldn't care less. I even helped them on one occasion, correcting a publicity ad in English.

I asked Siedlo if he knew someone at the Argentine consulate who could hasten a permanent visa for me. "Let's go see," he said. So off we went to the consulate where we spoke with a vice-consul,

165

who treated me like royalty and stamped my passport with a permanent resident visa. I was glad to be entering Argentina again as newborn, because my old permanent visa was in my old passport and now I would not have to explain why I had never informed immigration why I had become a resident of another country and would not have taxation problems, something I had become most wary of. The trip to Buenos Aires on Swissair was Geneva-Zurich-Buenos Aires. Jeanne accompanied me as far as Zurich, where she had something to do. While still in the air she said something I remember well: o*n one hand I am sorry that you are leaving; on the other hand, I am glad because I know that your heart is there.* I didn't realize how true those words were until much later.

Buenos Aires

I arrived in Buenos Aires well rested after twelve hours in Swissair's care and took a taxi directly to a 5-star hotel in Downtown Buenos Aires. The costs of this transfer were on IATA this time. Nevertheless, I didn't want to stay in the hotel very long. I had to find a place. I checked the newspapers' classified ads and soon found an ideal three-room apartment with an ample kitchen and bathroom in the Belgrano neighborhood, about fifteen minutes to downtown by car, somewhat longer by public transportation. The building was set back about a hundred yards in a garden and had a large balcony. But it was full of old furniture. I told the estate agent that I'd take it, but only if it was empty of furniture, and I'd pay a US$ rent. The owner couldn't resist. My furniture arrived from Geneva, and I moved in.

I also had to find an office and hire a secretary. I lucked out again with both. I found an office (it was actually a two-room apartment easily turned into an office) across from Buenos Aires's beautiful Plaza San Martín. I placed an ad in the Buenos Aires Herald for a bilingual secretary and received about a half-dozen replies, for whom I scheduled interviews. The obvious winner was the Pepsi Cola director's secretary, who said she was looking for different employment mostly because she was too busy in her present one. I told her that she would have a lot of free time with us, which turned out to not be the case, but I believed it then. But her main problem was whether the employment was permanent and whether we would be paying social services such as retirement. I had to admit that there was nothing permanent involved because I truly had no idea how long we (I) would be functioning in Argentina — and that I had no intention of paying for social services, mostly because of the bureaucracy involved. She left.

I finally chose María Teresa Gutiérrez, who knew the English language better than I and spoke it with only a slight accent, was a translator and teacher of English to Argentine executives. When going through the notes I had made about the ones I interviewed for the job and came to her name, I had written "Not a secretary but I like her." It was true that she had no experience as a secretary (but she became an excellent one) and I certainly did like her, a lot.

I am going into a certain amount of detail about this because M.T. (as I called her then and still do), and I fell in love, partnered and had a son whom we named Nicolás Gawain. Gawain because I had recently read *Sir Gawain and the Green Knight* and felt that this new baby would be like him, which turned out to be at least partly true — in my humble opinion. And Nicolás in case he doesn't like being called Gawain when he grows up. However, everybody still calls him Gawain 34 years later and he quite likes it.

Seminario Pedagógico Waldorf

There were still only two Waldorf schools in Argentina. I thought I knew the reason for that, one of the reasons anyway: Insistence by German teachers and non-teachers that in order to be a Waldorf teacher, one had to attend the Waldorf teacher's seminar in Germany. But in practice in order to do that the applicant would have to have the resources to be able to travel to Germany, take an intensive course to learn German, which would take a minimum of six months, more likely a year, then a full-time, five days a week, teacher-training course. Unlikely. The result was that there were few qualified teachers and no new schools.

I had had direct experience with the Waldorf schools in Switzerland and Germany, as well as with the teachers. I saw that some were excellent teachers and others, a minority I hoped, were hopeless despite having graduated from the seminar. I came to the conclusion that, although the seminar was necessary, more important is the human quality of the individual as well as his or her dedication to Waldorf education and anthroposophy. I also realized that an Argentinean school would necessarily be different from a German one — just as their cultures in general are different. In any case, they would not be German.

I called Elena Wedeltoft, one of the main co-founders of the San Miguel Arcángel school, who was still a teacher there. (Several years later, with the intention of retiring, she moved with her family to a town further away from Buenos Aires, still a bit more rural. But once there, the local population asked to *please* found a Waldorf school there. She finally agreed and thus was born the *Escuela Clara de Asis*. Perhaps one day one of her children will write a biography.) I said, "How about founding a Waldorf teacher training seminar?" It took about ten seconds of consideration for her to reply, "Of course."

The first meeting to found the *Seminario Pedagógico Waldorf* took place in mid-April 1989 in the Anthroposophical Society Argentina's building. I remember the day well, because Nicolás Gawain was born on April 15, 1989.

With María Teresa and Gawain.

I had also invited Beatriz Artuso, a co-founder and teacher at the Escuela San Jean in Buenos Aires. She came with Ursula Vallendor, who became a member of our Coordination Group, and a tireless organizer and teacher of teachers at various new Waldorf school around the country.

We started giving class at the Sociedad Antroposófica's building, but soon changed to the Rudolf Steiner school — of all places — in Florida. It was over two decades since we had abandoned that school and it had changed very much since then. It was ideal for the seminar because our classes were from 6 to 9 P.M. And we could use the school's classrooms. Teachers from the two existing schools with years of experience acted as teachers on the various aspects of Waldorf education. I taught "sociology," which consisted of Steiner's social tri-formation or threefold society concept and *The Philosophy of Freedom*. I considered myself competent to teach the threefold society, especially because it was totally unknown to the students.

This takes me back to when I first moved to Switzerland in 1974. In Dornach and in Achberg I heard many "experts" speak on the subject and read articles about it. But they were all academic, that is, economists, philosophers, political scientists, Waldorf teachers, and so on. Missing, in my judgment, were people who were actually active in economic activity — employees of large firms, entrepreneurs, management, etc. I was active in an important economic organization, IATA, a trade organization of practically all the world's international airlines. I saw how the threefold idea could apply to that industry and be beneficial to all concerned. Theory is fine to understand, but only practical experience can show how it can or cannot be applied in real life.

I wrote an open letter to a magazine specializing in the threefold society concept inviting readers *active* in economic life and interested in the threefold society to contact me. I was surprised at the number of people who replied, about a dozen. I called for a meeting at a certain place and time (don't remember the place or time) and some very interesting people, mostly German and two Swiss — all men, as expected in 1974, and all working in economic, profit-making companies — responded to the call. We agreed to meet three times a year, spring autumn and winter, with the objective of discussing how to make the threefold society a practical reality. One of the original members, Klaus Hartwig, resigned from the group when he retired, saying that he

170

was no longer "active in economic life," and so no longer can be a member. As far as I know he was the only one that resigned for that reason. Many of the other original members simply ran out of time on earth. Amazingly enough, that group has been meeting ever since — a half a century. At the moment there are still seven members including me, although I no longer attend the meetings.

Rear: Michael Schreyer, Urs Vogt, Werner Rieger, Klaus Hartwig. Front: Frank T Smith, Alexander Finkh, Heinrich Köhler, Hanspeter Bühler, Fritz Otto.

The Philosophy of Freedom was another kettle of fish. I found myself teaching about philosophy without knowing much about the subject. I had read Philosophy of Freedom (POF) and thought I understood it. But Steiner refers to other philosophers in the book who were little more than names to me. I had read and liked and admired Plato and had read excerpts from other authors, including Karl Marx. But my public education through high school in New York and some college afterward did not include philosophy, not a word. Nevertheless, although all of my seminar students had at least finished secondary school and some college in Argentina, they were as ignorant of philosophy as I was, or more so. I had a three-week course with them, an hour a day, five days a week. I soon realized that they had no idea of what Rudolf Steiner, or I were talking about.

Luckily a book titled *Sophie's World* by Jostein Gaarder, a Norwegian, fell into my hands. It's fiction, but within the story he teaches Sophie about philosophy through the Renaissance, Romanticism and Existentialism, as well as Darwinism and Karl Marx. From that time on I spent at least the first week, sometimes longer, on the History of Philosophy before tackling Rudolf Steiner. The result was that both the students and I learned how to understand *Philosophy of Freedom*.

The seminario grew and graduated more and more new teachers and the number of Waldorf schools in Argentina grew as well and is still growing.

Lai Reborn

One day MT and I were in our office in Buenos Aires, when someone knocked. The door was always on a snap-lock because, well, Buenos Aires isn't the safest city in the world. MT checked, the guy looked strange but was alone and not dangerous looking, so she let him in. It was Laimonis Holms! But a different version. I hadn't seen or heard from him in many years, and I may not have recognized him if he hadn't smiled that charming smile and said, in accented English, "Hello Frank, how are you?" There was no suit and tie this time though, not even close. He had a beard, and his hair reached his shoulders, he wore a wrinkled shirt and trousers that didn't look very clean, and sandals. He had quit Air France because he was finally fed up with the dog-eat-dog business world and now lived happily in a hippy town, San Marcos Sierra, in the province of Córdoba and had come to Buenos Aires because he needed to work for two more years in order to qualify for a social security pension. Argentina required at least thirty years of contributions to qualify.

"You don't have something for me by any chance, Frank?" he asked after the greetings and hugs and having explained his pension problem. And, as destiny decreed, at that moment I did have something for him, if I could clear it with the director in Geneva, which I thought I could. The local tariff integrity airlines group was just getting off the ground, so to speak, but more was missing than the fines we used to apply for discounting sins and the non-participation of the U.S. airlines. It was more like the meeting of a club than a serious attempt to self-control the market. I was thinking of getting the funds from Geneva to buy test tickets, like in the old days. But who's to buy them? It had to be someone reliable, honest, capable and, preferably, who understands what he's doing. And in walks Lai Holms, an experienced airline guy, but long enough ago so that travel agency employees would not recognize him.

After getting the go-ahead from Geneva, I loaned Lai the money to get a haircut and buy a decent-looking suit and tie. I forgot one thing though: an attaché-case, a necessary element of the businessman's wardrobe those days. I sent him out to travel agencies to look for discounts to major European cities. He did well. During the week he bought three test tickets on different airlines to different destinations. He received offers on Argentine Airlines, but I left them out. Previously, when we were still imposing fines, it was so easy to get discounts on AA that they threatened to leave IATA. So, I made a confidential deal: if I bought a test ticket on AA, I would also buy one on another carrier to the same destination. This would allow the sales manager to tell his superior, an air force general, that he had no choice but to give discounts because the foreign competition was offering them. Now, with the ones Lai bought, we could have easily bought one or more from AA without a guilty conscience.

María Teresa, Lai and I went separately to the Tariff Integrity meeting of the Board of Airline Representatives on the other side of town from our office (I forget why). When all were present, I introduced Laimonis Holms as my new assistant, adding that he was previously Air France's sales manager, but that was over ten years ago. M.T. was present to make an accurate record of the proceedings. I needed that to send to Geneva in order to prove that I was indeed doing my job. I would also send copies to the representatives present for them to forward to their head offices, from whom they had received instructions to cooperate with IATA's Tariff Integrity representative.

"You aren't by chance related to Sherlock, Mr Holms?" a wiseguy cracked. But Lai was used to it: "No," Lai smiled, "he has an 'e' after Holms, I don't." Good one. I asked him to please show the evidence of discounts he had obtained in the form of test tickets. He raised a plastic shopping bag from below the table which I hadn't noticed. "My God," one of them shouted, "a shopping bag full! Did you buy them in a supermarket?" (all laugh.)

Lai smiled and said he had bought them from travel agencies, but the prices could have come from a supermarket. The first was an Air Canada round trip ticket from Buenos Aires to Rome with a connection in Toronto at a twenty percent discount. The Alitalia manager stood up and cried histrionically "What? Air Canada?"

Lufthansa: "All roads lead to Rome."

Alitalia: "But not via Toronto." (general merriment, including we IATA folks). The Air Canada guy said what they all say: "I'll have to find out from my sales manager how this could have happened."

But it was all a bluff, something we all knew, so tariff integrity's days were numbered. Finally, Brian Maine, that fancy dancer in the Head Office halls, came up with an even better idea to save our jobs, including his own: "fraud prevention." Yeah! And it worked. There was plenty of fraud in the airline/travel agent business, and it was something that kept me busy. By that time Lai had completed the time needed for his pension so he could return to the wilderness of Cordoba, then the mountains of Jujuy and the natural life. It did him good obviously, because he was 96 years old when he died over 35 years later.

Fraud Prevention

Fraud prevention wasn't only such obvious things as identifying stolen tickets. The fraudsters were always a step or two ahead. I could describe some interesting examples of ingenious methods they invented without getting caught. As soon as I could think of a way to frustrate them, they moved on to a different scheme.

One day in 1991 Brian Mayne called me with the news that IATA had a new Finance Director. I told him I already knew that and what else is new.

"What's new, Frank, is that he's decided to close the Buenos Aires fraud prevention office." He paused to let it sink in. "You will be transferred to Montreal," (IATA had another head office in Montreal in order to be near the Civil Aviation Board. In fact, Montreal was the original head office, but when the airlines were recruiting Knut Hammarskjöld to be Director General, he said sure, but not in Montreal, gotta be Geneva, where he now lives. As Dag's nephew and an ex-government air transport official in Sweden he had a lot of clout, so they opened a second IATA head office in Geneva. At least that's the legend; why else would we have two head offices? "You will be Assistant Director Fraud Prevention Western Hemisphere with a raise in salary because the cost of living is higher there than in Argentina," Brian added.

I had been in Montreal once for a meeting and the impression I got was everything worked, not like in Argentina where very little worked as it should, but that it was bitter cold up there. I thought of the Hammarskjöld legend and said, "Not Montreal, gotta be

Geneva." I thought he'd laugh, but he surprised me by saying "I think I can arrange that." Then: "Think it over, talk it over with your wife and let me know soon. You have enough time in and age for early retirement you know. Oh, by the way, there's no point in arguing with the Financial Director. He's made up his mind, period, to quote him."

I didn't know about the early retirement option, but I soon found out. Yes, I could retire early (I was only 58) at a reduced pension. I asked María Teresa and she said, "Let's go." But that was just a first reaction. Upon thinking it over we came to a different conclusion. Moving to the North Pole with a two-year-old baby and finding a place to live where rents (and everything else) is much more expensive, and with a different language, I'd be working in a 9 to 5 environment again and in the new kind of building which doesn't even have offices. In Geneva I at least had a private office to hide in. The last time I visited there though everything had been converted into a zoo, also known as cubicles. Furthermore, being theoretically responsible for the whole Western Hemisphere — alone, I'd be living in an airplane.

Just then a new economy minister had decided that the only way to control hyperinflation was to peg the Argentine peso to the U.S. dollar. He called it the "convertibility plan." It worked for a while, but a much longer while than I had foreseen. With the peso having the same value as the dollar, I lost the dollar advantage. It lasted until 2002. If we had known, it would last so long we might have opted for Montreal. Luckily, we didn't know.

On the plus side for staying in Argentina was that I was quite active in running and teaching in the Waldorf Teachers Seminario. I was also doing some preparatory work in organization development consultancy. Now I would be able to dedicate much more time to that, as well as giving English lessons to advanced businesspeople in small groups. So, we decided to stay in Argentina and retire from the first world. **Good choice.**

176

Result: the seminario, the consultancy and the English lessons went well, until one day two pwople came to my office in the Therapeutikum (Anthroposophical Medical Center) in Buenos Aires. The Therapeutikum was not related to the seminario, but I helped the doctors organize the Therapeutikum and themselves and somehow work together. Doctors are essentially authoritarian; they tell the patient what to do, nothing democratic about it. So it's hard for them to work together. My office there also housed "Eco Asociados," consultants. We were four people, but the other three still had to work in their day-jobs, so didn't have time for much else. We did, however, discuss the projects I was undertaking, and I gladly listened to their advice, which was often helpful.

Traslasierra

One of the two people who walked into my office that day told me that she lived in the Traslasierra Valley in the Province of Córdoba, and she and other families living there were interested in starting a Waldorf school for their children. She didn't know much about Waldorf education, but a friend, Yasmine Antonio, my primary school pupil and Waldorf teachers seminario student, had told her about it. I had been there twice, once during my time in Argentina between 1962 and 1974, and once this time. Mario Durán, one of the first parents of the San Miguel Arcángel school, owned a small inn in Nono, one of the valley's towns, and it was him we had visited. I knew it as a remote but beautiful mountainous area about a thousand kilometers west of Buenos Aires. I was surprised that there were families there interested in Waldorf education. Although the tourist industry had grown somewhat in more recent times, Traslasierra was practically unknown in Buenos Aires. Gradually, more and more people from larger cities moved there to escape the big cities' pressure and enjoy nature.

I told the young lady that if they wanted a Waldorf school, the first thing they would need was teachers. So, they should send two future teachers, if possible, to Buenos Aires to attend the Seminario Waldorf. After completing the two-year course, they would be prepared to return to the Traslasierra Valley and start a school. She smiled, shook her head and said they couldn't do that. I don't recall more details of the conversation, only that I said I would be willing to go there in the summer for vacation and speak to the interested parents. I thought that if the project looked realistic, I might convince an experienced Waldorf teacher to move there, or at least a graduate of the Seminario.

María Teresa, Gawain and I went to the Traslasierra Valley that summer. My new contacts there arranged for us to stay at the Estancia Holandesa, owned by a Dutch family who immigrated to Argentina the previous generation. It had a large room, perhaps once a ballroom, perfect for a meeting. I spoke about Waldorf education, the schools in Buenos Aires (the only ones) and implied that if they really wanted such a school for their children, it was up to them. There were of course many questions, but the main one was the last: How much would it cost to send a child to such a school? The one-to-one peso/dollar convertibility system was still in effect, so one peso was worth one U.S. dollar. In Buenos Aires the schools were charging 300 pesos a month. I thought most things were cheaper here in Traslasierra, so I said about 100 pesos a month. The faces dropped, and I realized that if there even was a school, a problem would be financing it. A third party watching would most likely have said that we were all wasting our time. There were children, but there was no land, no schoolhouse and no teachers. It didn't look promising. Nevertheless, I had hope and I saw and felt that most of the parents did as well. Their hope, however, was centered on me at the moment. What to do? A choice was coming on.

The deciding moment came when Omar Bare and Ivon decided to donate their property, a two-hectare field — once a wheat-field

— with a small house on it, where the kindergarten could start. They called it "el trigal." At first, I thought it might have something to do with a tripartite society. But no, it means wheat-field in Spanish. Still, it does kind of ring a bell. It would do for a kindergarten to start with. It was 1997 and the teacher was Alejandra de Lellis, helped by some mothers: Marian, Inés, Mavi, Ivón, Flor.

María Teresa and I now had to decide whether to leave Buenos Aires and the really convenient apartment we had in the Belgrano section in order to dive into the (almost) unknown planet of Traslasierra. Gawain was in the second grade at the Rudolf Steiner Schule, so a question was whether the Escuela El Trigal was going to exist or not. Also, if we could sell the apartment for a reasonable price, that is, enough to buy something adequate on the other end. I, by the way, was already 65 years old. María Teresa was sixteen years younger but was hesitant to leave her aged parents. A choice had to be made though, and somehow, I felt — not merely reasoned, but felt — that it had to be to go to Traslasierra and la Escuela El Trigal.

I asked the students graduating from the seminario if someone would like to go to the Traslasierra valley in Córdoba and be the first teacher at a new school there, with no guarantee of success or if the school would even really be born.

We sold the apartment in Belgrano and headed for La Población, the village where Fleur de Wet (South African) and Rafael Barragán lived, and stayed with them for a few days, until we found a house to rent in a neighboring village. They had a son, Ciro, the same age as Gawain, future school compañeros.

I had prepared the statute, or bylaws of the new school's civil association: "Comunidad Educativa El Trigal," to be registered with the provincial justice system and education authorities, a necessity in order to avoid legal chaos. It was basically the same as the San Miguel Arcángel statute with the names and location changed. A meeting was called of the prospective parents and teachers in order to found the civil association, approve the statute, and elect an executive committee. I asked someone to read the statute out loud. I was surprised to hear it. I objected that it was not the statute I had prepared. It only mentioned the association's attribute to found and operate a school, whereas I had clearly indicated schools practicing Waldorf pedagogy. The spokesperson for a small group said that by changing it we would be free to use the best of various methods instead of only Waldorf. For example, Krishnamurti and Sai Baba.

I don't remember exactly what I said, but I was not happy. Basically, I must have said that with no disrespect for either of the two persons named (in fact, I had a high opinion of Krishnamurti), neither of them had founded a real educational movement, nor did they describe a particular pedagogy. On the other hand, there were already several Waldorf schools in Buenos Aires as well as a two-year teacher training course. That there were also many such schools worldwide, especially in Germany (where the first school was founded in 1919), Switzerland, Holland and Scandinavia. They are known to assist new schools in third-world countries, even financially. In short, it will be a Waldorf oriented school or none at all, at least not with me. By acclamation those present agreed that it would be a Waldorf school. Even the statute manipulators agreed, probably when financing was brought up.

Gladys Miranda, a recent graduate of the Seminario Pedagógico Waldorf, arrived with her husband and two sons to be the new school's first teacher. Her older son, Pedro, was Gawain's age and the other, Pablo, a few years younger. The Escuela El Trigal opened in March 1998 with two grades, first and third, in a combined class, and ten children ... total! They were in the same and only house in which the kindergarten still functioned. It was obvious that more room was needed for classrooms. One of the parents, Mario Siskindovich, was an architect and designed a clever, practical school, with a new classroom being built as needed every year.

María Teresa and I also worked as teachers. M.T., a professional, taught English for eight years. I, non-professionally but with experience, for a much shorter period, including baseball — in English of course: "Three strikes and you're out!"

Ciro, Gawain and Pedro building El Trigal's the first classroom.

While we were in the pioneer stage of development, I was a little more equal among equals as far as administration went. When over the years the school grew and entered the bureaucratic stage, many new people became involved, especially parents, but teachers as well, who wanted to do something that I didn't agree with: continue to expand into a secondary school. In Argentina that was, and is, from grades 7 through 12. I was able to avoid it for several years, because I knew the dangers of premature expansion. Eventually however, there was a great deal of pressure from both parents and teachers. Before finally acceding, I asked each teacher, from kindergarten to sixth grade, if they wanted El Trigal to have a secondary school. The answer was either yes or "why not?"

I was wary of a secondary school mostly because I remembered what happened many years before to the Colegio Saint Jean in Buenos Aires, which soon became an ex- Waldorf school once it expanded prematurely. However, by around 2014 there was so much desire for El Trigal to expand that, although I probably could have delayed it for a while longer, I didn't want to become that classical original founder of an organization who hangs on beyond his time and opposes progress. So, I gradually stepped back, if not completely down, and the secondary school became a reality.

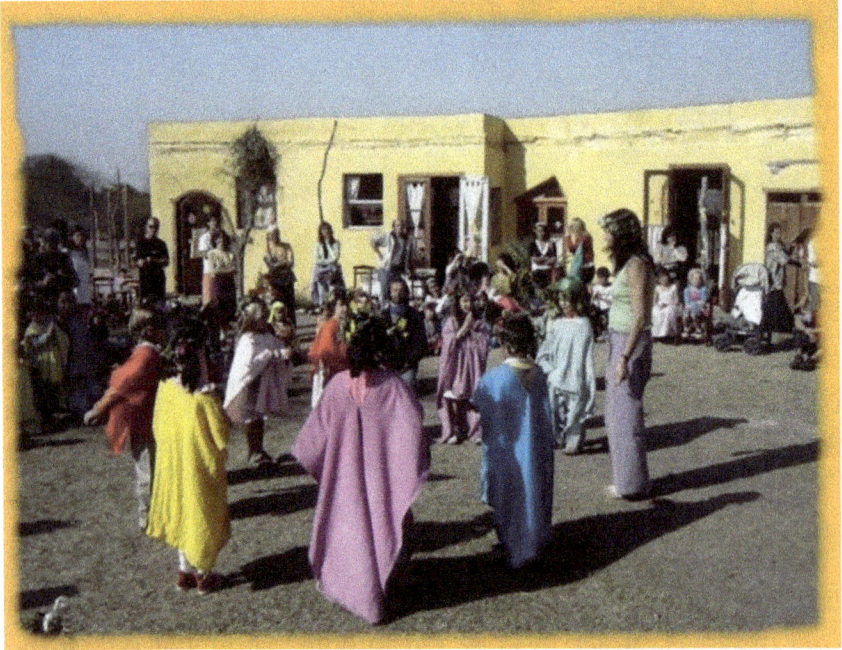

The El Trigal school in the early years.

The number of so-called Waldorf schools in Argentina has grown exponentially since then, especially if we include kindergartens and preparatory groups. I don't think we can attribute the growth to Waldorf education alone though. An important factor is the poor quality of public schools. During one of the early years an *inspectora* from the provincial education ministry in Córdoba was visiting and we invited her to a parent's meeting where one of the mothers led a circle-dance. The inspector said to all of us, including the parents: "We are aware that public education has failed; that's why I am so pleased with what you are doing here."

*

Twenty-four years ago, I began *SouthernCrossReview.org*, *a review of Anthroposophy, Fiction, Education, Science, Current Events, Essays, Book reviews and Poetry.* At first it appeared every two months, but times change. For the last several years we have been sending at least one article or story a week, anthroposophical or not, sometimes two. I say we, because the internet design and technical complications (much of it beyond me) is handled by my "tech guy" Gawain Smith. This photo shows that he is not a technical workaholic. He also practices his real love: music.

I have also been doing translations from German to English, mostly works by Rudolf Steiner, and publishing them. Steiner's First Class lectures have been published in German by the Rudolf Steiner Estate since 1977. They were sold, however, only to "responsible" individuals. (I have number 128.) When Rudolf Steiner's literary work entered the public domain 75 years after his death in 2000, they became available to everyone, in German. Translations in other languages were still protected by copyright laws though and were exclusively in the hands of so-called "readers" officially approved by the General Anthropsophical Society in Dornach. The readers guard them with an anthroposophical top-secret classification, to the extent that they only read them to members of the "Free University for Spiritual Science." I found the whole thing ridiculous and unfair because many non-German speaking individuals, members or simply those interested in anthroposophy, were also interested in what Steiner had to say about his school for initiation. At that time when he was giving the lessons of the School, it was only for members, but he never finished even the First Class before his death, when his intention was for three classes. But the Society claims that the School still exists by the mere act of reading the texts of his lectures. Whether the School exists or not, access to the Class lessons should not be restricted, when it is readily available to anyone in German. Rudolf Steiner was only 64 years old when he died. Many think he was poisoned. I used to doubt it, but have come to consider it possible, even probable.

In addition to translations, I have also written many stories and even some books.

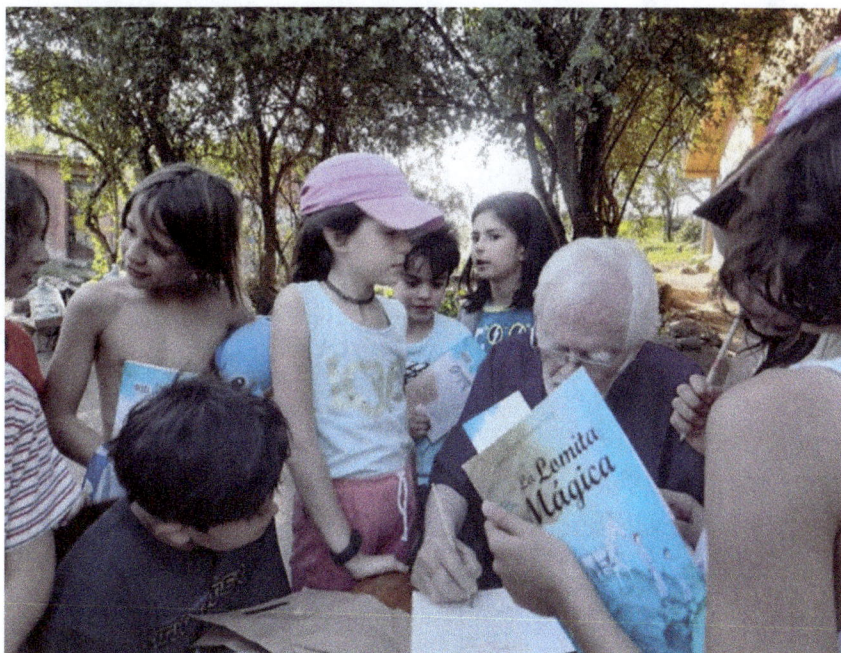

The author meets with his fans from the Escuela Dandelion (Córdoba) who came to the Escuela El Trigal to visit.

Conclusion

After reading what I have written above, I must conclude that I have been exceedingly fortunate and have made many good choices, if only because they turned out to be first steps leading to positive outcomes — albeit unconsciously — and some bad ones as well. So, I can only agree with Bernard Lievegoed when he said many years ago "We are the fortunate ones." I am without doubt one of the fortunate ones.

Like Lievegoed, I include having Anthroposophy for being responsible to a large extent. The world today is, after all, very materialistic. I do not pretend to be particularly spiritual, but at least I have concluded, thanks to anthroposophy, that a spiritual world exists, must exist in order for life to have meaning. Such meaning must also include reincarnation, for the simple reason that one life is not sufficient for the necessary development within a spiritual as well as a physical world.

Can I prove it to others? Of course not, that would be too easy. As Einstein said, "God doesn't play dice." He doesn't make life on earth easy either. Niels Bohr replied: "Einstein, stop telling God what to do."

When we — Renate, Bibi and I — left New York for Buenos Aires in 1962, I never for one minute suspected that I would never return to the United States, except on occasional short visits. Since then, I have lived in Argentina, Switzerland, Germany, back to Switzerland, and back again, finally, to Argentina. I have always been a foreigner, not in forced exile, but in exile, nevertheless. I may have looked like the natives of those countries, but my accent always gave me away. I learned their languages, but never perfectly nor accent free.

Exile's End

In exile I am from this place and that,
So let me tell you a thing I have learned:
All men are exiles and heavy of heart,
The price of a ticket to their ancestral home
Requires a lifetime of arduous travel.
I choose to presume, along with the rest,
That exile won't last much longer than death.

On-Line Activities

Throughout the text, there have been several references to books, lectures, articles or other on-line resources. Here you will find the actual links and URLs to be used should you want to access them.

Contacting the Publisher:
https://www.elib.com/eMail/AnthroPubs/

Anthroposophical Publications website:
https://AnthroposophicalPublications.org/

The Gospel of Luke
https://wn.rudolfsteinerelib.org/Lectures/GA114/English/RSP1964/GosLuk_index.html

Die Kernpunkte der sozialen Frage
https://wn.rudolfsteinerelib.org/Books/GA023/German/GA023_index.html

Basic Issues of the Social Question
https://wn.rudolfsteinerelib.org/Books/GA023/English/SCR2001/GA023_index.html

Toward A Threefold Society
https://wn.rudolfsteinerelib.org/Books/GA023/English/eLib2019/GA023_index.html

Favela Children
https://anthro.pub/books/favela-children/?swcfpc=1

The Philosophy of Freedom
https://rudolfsteinerelib.org/Books/GA004/

Southern Cross Review
https://SouthernCrossReview.org/

OTHER BOOKS

authored or translated by
Frank Thomas Smith
All titles available at your favorite Bookstore.

ANTHROPOSOPHICAL FANTASIES (by Roberto Fox, as told to Frank Thomas Smith): Anthroposophy, also known as Spiritual Science, is not known for fantastic literature, or fiction at all. So how can stories with titles like "Life on Mars," or "The Girl in the Floppy Hat," or "To Hunt a Nazi" qualify as anthroposophical. They do not — until now. Therefore, this book is groundbreaking. You may smile at times, even laugh; other stories may cause a lump in your throat ...

ISBN: 978-1948302104

ANTHROPOSOPHICAL GUIDELINES (Rudolf Steiner, translated by Frank Thomas Smith): this volume contains a collection of short essays by Steiner for the members of the Anthroposophical Society. They were written near the end of Steiner's life and in a way summarize, in highly concentrated form, the whole of anthroposophy. Each essay ends with a short summary of its contents, and these are known, in this translation, as the "guidelines." The guidelines are mantras and can be used quite fruitfully for meditation. Frank Thomas Smith provides a new, reinvigorated translation of Rudolf Steiner's classic, "Anthroposophical Leading Thoughts."

ISBN: 978-1948302418

CORONAVIRUS PANDEMIC II (by Judith von Halle, translated by Frank Thomas Smith): In this book, the main focus is not on the distressing social developments that have arisen as consequence of the coronavirus pandemic – and for good reason: Although there are already (thankfully) many quality descriptions and articles about this complex of problems and questions, at the same time on the other hand a dangerous knowledge-vacuum has arisen. Therefore, in this book I will refrain from elaborating on the problems already made widely visible in favor of this knowledge-vacuum, which will be outlined as an addition to what has already been described in Vol. I.

ISBN: 978-1948302357

ESOTERIC LESSONS FOR THE FIRST CLASS Volumes I, II, and III (Rudolf Steiner, translated by Frank Thomas Smith): During the re-founding of the Anthroposophical Society at Christmas 1923, Rudolf Steiner also reconstituted the 'Esoteric School' which had originally functioned in Germany from 1904 until 1914, when the outset of the First World War made it's continuance impossible. Twenty-eight lectures in three Volumes with in-line illustrations and blackboard drawings.

ISBN: 978-1948302289 (vol. 1)
978-1948302302 (vol. 2)
978-1948302333 (vol. 3)

189

FAVELA CHILDREN (by Ute Craemer, translated by Frank Thomas Smith): Ute Craemer is an educator and social worker who has dedicated over fifty years of her life to teaching and nurturing the poor children of the favelas (slums) in Brazil. As an experienced Waldorf teacher, she has been able to understand the needs of the children and their families and provide them with the spiritual nourishment they cry out for. Favela Children is a moving and informative account of Ute Craemer's social work in the favelas and of her personal development ...

ISBN: 978-1948302425

THE HISTORY AND ACTUALITY OF IMPERIALISM (Rudolf Steiner, translated by Frank Thomas Smith): In 1920 Rudolf Steiner had already foreseen that the future imperialism would be economic rather than military or nationalistic. In these three lectures he describes the history of imperialism from ancient times to the present and into the future. The Anglo-American would play an increasingly important role in future developments, so the English visitors who attended must have been especially attentive.

ISBN: 978-1948302203

JOURNEY TO THE STARS (by Frank Thomas Smith): The protagonists of these 12 stories are involved in fascinating adventures, which will delight young readers and leave an indelible impression on their minds and hearts. For children from 9 years old on up.

ISBN: 978-1948302395

LOVE IN THE LIFE OF SPIES (by Frank Thomas Smith). is, as its title suggests, a love story between two spies during the Cold War, an East German woman and an American man, each working for their respective opposing clandestine agencies and, therefore, against each other. Their meetings, seemingly accidental, unfold over years in the United States, Germany, Argentina, Paraguay and, finally, serve only to reveal an uncertain future. It asks the question: is such a love viable under such complicated and adverse geopolitical circumstances? Or was it meant to be – at least as a possibility – according to karma's blueprint. The answer, although not definitive, is maybe, or even yes involving, strangely enough, Anthroposophy.

ISBN: 978-1948302517

THE MAGIC MOUND (by Frank Thomas Smith): Sergio and his younger brother, Divino are poor children who live in a favela (slum) in Sao Paulo, Brazil. They go on vacation with their revered teacher, doña Ute (pronounced oo-teh), to the country house of one of Ute's friends. Once there, they leave the house together to fetch kindling wood. They cross a stream and discover a strange round mound surrounded by white stones ... for children from 9 years old on up.

ISBN: 978-1948302258

REINCARNATION BLUES, AND OTHER POEMS, is a collection of 49 poems, cantos, sonnets, and poetic stories, all a product of the fertile mind of Frank Thomas Smith. Also included are other author's poems that have been translated by Frank.

ISBN: 978-1948302555

THE TALKING TREES / LOS ÁRBOLES PARLANTES (by Frank Thomas Smith): Alma and Nico live on opposite ends of a forest near their homes. One day when they are both reading the same book (The Magic Mound) within the forest, but far from each other, the trees suddenly talk to them. A bilingual edition for children from 9 years old on up.

ISBN: 978-1948302715

TOWARD A THREEFOLD SOCIETY (Rudolf Steiner, translated by Frank Thomas Smith): This work, written late in the life of Rudolf Steiner, makes use of a threefold analysis of the human individual and of human society. Man as an individual, or in a group, functions basically in three modes: thinking/perceiving, feeling/valuing, and willing/planning/acting. A unit of functioning, whether a part of an individual or part of a society has its proper role. Each role needs a certain respect from other areas if it is to function properly ...

ISBN: 978-1948302166

AND MORE ...